KU-266-871

WITHDRAWN

514237

H~~WITHDRAWN~~

the Media

PRINCIPLES AND PRACTICES
FOR HEALTH PROMOTION

CARI...

SM 8008041
WA
590
EFG
H P
7day
loan

√

WITHDRAWN
SM...

007 470 0006

Health and the Media

PRINCIPLES AND PRACTICES FOR HEALTH PROMOTION

Garry Egger MPH, PhD

Director, Centre for Health Promotion & Research, Sydney, NSW
Clinical Lecturer, Centre for Health Advancement, School of Medicine, University of Newcastle

Robert J. Donovan BPsych, PhD

Associate Professor of Marketing, Department of Management, and Co-Director,
Health Promotion Development and Evaluation Program, University of Western Australia

Chairman, Donovan Research, Marketing and Communications Research Consultants,
Perth, Western Australia

Ross Spark BEd, BA, MSc

Director, Tropical Public Health Unit, Peninsula and Torres Strait Regional
Health Authority, Cairns, Queensland

Scientist, Cancer Prevention Research Centre, Faculty of Medicine, University of Queensland

McGRAW-HILL BOOK COMPANY Sydney

New York San Francisco Auckland Bogotá
Caracas Lisbon London Madrid Mexico City
Milan Montreal New Delhi San Juan
Singapore Tokyo Toronto

NOTICE
Medicine is an ever-changing science. As new research and clinical experience broaden our knowledge, changes in treatment and drug therapy are required. The editors and the publisher of this work have checked with sources believed to be reliable in their efforts to provide information that is complete and generally in accord with the standards accepted at the time of publication. However, in view of the possibility of human error or changes in medical sciences, neither the editor, nor the publisher, nor any other party who has been involved in the preparation or publication of this work warrants that the information contained herein is in every respect accurate or complete. Readers are encouraged to confirm the information contained herein with other sources. For example and in particular, readers are advised to check the product information sheet included in the package of each drug they plan to administer to be certain that the information contained in this book is accurate and that changes have not been made in the recommended dose or in the contraindications for administration. This recommendation is of particular importance in connection with new or infrequently used drugs.

Text © 1993, Garry Egger, Rob Donovan and Ross Spark
Illustrations and design © 1993 McGraw-Hill Book Company Australia Pty Limited

Apart from any fair dealing for the purposes of study, research, criticism or review, as permitted under the *Copyright Act*, no part may be reproduced by any process without written permission. Enquiries should be made to the publisher, marked for the attention of the Permissions Editor, at the address below.

Copying for educational purposes
Under the copying provisions of the *Copyright Act*, copies of parts of this book may be made by an educational institution. An agreement exists between the Copyright Agency Limited (CAL) and the relevant educational authority (Department of Education, university, TAFE, etc.) to pay a licence fee for such copying. It is not necessary to keep records of copying except where the relevant educational authority has undertaken to do so by arrangement with the Copyright Agency Limited.

For further information on the CAL licence agreements with educational institutions, contact the Copyright Agency Limited, Level 19, 157 Liverpool Street, Sydney NSW 2000. Where no such agreement exists, the copyright owner is entitled to claim payment in respect of any copies made.

Enquiries concerning copyright in McGraw-Hill publications should be directed to the Permissions Editor at the address below.

National Library of Australia Cataloguing-in-Publication data:

Egger, Garry.
Health and the media: principles and practices for health promotion.

Bibliography
Includes index.
ISBN 0 07 470000 6.

1. Health promotion. 2. Mass media in health education. I. Donovan, Rob. II. Spark, Ross. III. Title.

613

Published in Australia by
McGraw-Hill Book Company Australia Pty Limited
4 Barcoo Street, Roseville NSW 2069, Australia
Typeset in Australia by DOCUPRO, Sydney
Printed in Australia by McPherson's Printing Pty Limited

514237

Contents

About the authors

Garry Egger MPH, PhD

Dr Garry Egger has been involved in health promotion since 1972, and has worked on a number of major media campaigns ranging from drink driving to abdominal obesity in men. He has written numerous scientific articles and 12 books on health, including the text *Health Promotion Strategies and Methods* (with Ross Spark and Jim Lawson). He is currently Director of the Centre for Health Promotion and Research in Sydney and a Clinical Lecturer in the School of Medicine at the University of Newcastle.

Robert J. Donovan BPsych, PhD

Dr Rob Donovan has held academic positions in Australia and the USA and has been a visiting scientist with the National AIDS Information and Education Program at the Center for Disease Control in Atlanta, Georgia. In 1974 he founded Donovan Research, a marketing and communications research company. Dr Donovan has a special interest and expertise in the areas of social marketing and communication and he has been involved in strategy and research in a variety of health and social policy areas for state and federal government departments.

Ross Spark BEd, BA, MSc

Ross Spark is a co-author of *Health Promotion Strategies and Methods* and he has been involved in health promotion in northern Australia for the past 10 years. Much of that time has been spent working with Aboriginal and Torres Strait Islander people. He is currently Director of the Tropical Public Health Unit in Cairns.

Acknowledgments

Sections of this book are based on materials developed for the Distance Learning Program of the Postgraduate Diploma in Health Promotion, Curtin University. This was a project supported by a grant from the Commonwealth Department of Health, Housing and Community Services under the National Health Promotion Program.

The authors wish to acknowledge comments and advice given on early drafts of this book by Dr Peter Howat of the Department of Health Promotion at Curtin University.

Thanks also go to Suzanne Wood for research assistance.

Introduction

*I*MPROVEMENTS IN the health of Australians in this century have occurred in three main phases (Hetzel & McMichael 1983). First, from the turn of the century to about 1950, there was a long period of increase in life expectancy, largely due to improvements in public health (Hinman 1990). In the second phase, from 1950 to 1970, there was a levelling of improvements from infectious diseases, but a rise in 'lifestyle related' diseases which, by the mid-1950s had surpassed infectious diseases as causes of death (Powles 1973). During the third phase, from 1970 to the present, there has been a recognition of, and greater emphasis on, these lifestyle causes. This phase has been characterised by the biggest improvements in longevity in history. Life expectancy increased from 68 to 73 years in men and from 74 to 80 years in women from 1960 to 1988 (Australian Bureau of Statistics 1990).

A good proportion of these improvements can be attributed to health promotion (Garrard 1992). Based on one conservative estimate, at least half of the improvement since 1960 (or a 16–19% decrease in mortality), can be attributed to some aspects of prevention or health promotion (Egger 1991). Holman (1992) has shown that in Western Australia, two-thirds of the 35 health-trend indicators set as prevention priorities since the early 1980s have improved by more than 10% in that time. Some of the major changes that have occurred in disease indices in Australia since 1960 are shown in the Table on page x.

What is health promotion?

HEALTH PROMOTION IS a relatively new discipline whose roots are grounded in both science and the arts. In its modern form, health promotion encompasses the more traditional 'health education' as well as other strategies which involve improvements to social and physical environments.

Much early health promotion focused on changing the behaviour of the individual—exhorting each individual or groups of individuals to make 'healthy choices'. More recently, an acknowledgment that many health gains that have occurred have been among the middle and upper socio-economic levels of society, has caused those involved to address the issue of equity in health and to investigate barriers to better health that exist among certain groups. This has led to different kinds of health promotion interventions—ones that seek to 'make the healthy choice the *easy* choice' through creating incentives and removing barriers to better health and, in some cases, through public health policy 'making the healthy choice the *only* choice'.

Recent changes in health patterns in Australia

Areas in which there have been marked improvements	*Areas in which there have been no improvements*
Overall mortality	Aboriginal health
Heart attack	Cancers
Stroke	pancreas
Injuries/poisonings	breast
motor vehicles	skin
drownings	lung (women)
falls	AIDS
occupational injury	Alcohol related diseases
Most infectious diseases	Asthma
Cancer of the lung (men)	Senile dementia
Cervical cancer (women)	STDs
Cancer of the stomach	Suicide in the young
Unintentional pregnancies	Violence/homicide
Pregnancy complications	Cirrhosis
Congenital abnormalities	Musculo-skeletal disorders
Dental health	
Perinatal complications	

A definition of health promotion which embraces this eclectic philosophy has been provided by Green and Kreuter (1990). Health promotion is '. . . the combination of educational and environmental supports for actions and conditions of living conducive to health'. In achieving the improvements in health gained through health promotion in recent times, a number of disciplines have been involved utilising a range of strategies. For example, engineers, legislators, advertisers and social scientists have reduced injury from road trauma by 50% since 1950 by changing freeway design, enforcing speed and seat belt laws, and providing widespread advertising and publicity about the risks of drinking and driving. Doctors, food scientists, exercise specialists and behavioural scientists have decreased deaths from heart disease by 50% since 1970 by promoting cessation of smoking, giving information about lifestyle changes, modifying the food supply and advertising new food choices. Epidemiologists, pharmacologists, doctors, sociologists, social workers and health educators have decreased the rate of death from infectious diseases by up to 70% by improving hygiene and living conditions, developing new immunisation techniques, quarantining, and increasing community awareness about infectious disease risks.

The media and health promotion

MASS MEDIA HAVE played a role in many of these improvements and in a number of ways: by *informing* about risks for developing heart disease, contracting AIDS, or being caught drinking and driving; by *motivating* individuals to quit smoking, take up exercise, alter their driving or sexual behaviour; and by *advocating* socio-political changes to social, structural and economic factors that affect exposure to cigarette smoking, access to exercise, or risk factors in the physical environment.

The use of the media is but one strategy in health promotion. There are many other strategies, as outlined in our previous book *Health Promotion Strategies and Methods* (Egger, Spark & Lawson 1990), and shown in the box (p. xii). No one strategy should be seen as the only approach, and others may, and indeed often should, be used independently of the mass media or in combination with them, depending on the circumstances. Additional references are available for different strategies, and these should be consulted in order to develop a broad approach to the field.

It should also be clear that although use of the media is a strategy in itself, various methods of media use are central to other strategy implementations. For example, the media can be used for increasing awareness of issues in community development, delivering information in patient education programs or informing about access to seminars for group processes. A knowledge of how to use the media is therefore a useful, if not essential, weapon in any health promotion practitioner's armoury.

Skills in developing media materials range from the relatively small-scale processes of writing a leaflet or carrying out a radio interview, to the conduct of a full-scale media advertising campaign. They require a knowledge of the different media and their uses in a variety of situations, and also a wide range of expertise: from journalism to graphic arts; from recording to production; from a knowledge of individual attitude-behaviour change models to social and political organisation.

No single practitioner could be expected to be an expert in all of the above strategies in health promotion. In use of the media alone, there is a variety of skills required that are difficult for any one individual to cover. In fact, it is often revealing to determine which medium a person is most skilled in, or whether she or he has any interest in, or aptitude for, media at all. Because health promotion requires communication, at least some of the skills necessary for the development of media materials are essential for anyone involved in health promotion.

This book not only gives information about the concepts and methods involved in using mass media in health promotion, but it also provides the reader with the practical skills required for actually using the media. In this respect, it is intended to complement other resources that aim to increase media skills.

Strategies in health promotion

A. *Focus on the individual*
    Patient education
    Medical and allied professional programs
    Home health care programs
    Programmed learning and self-help material
    Health promotion 'shopfronts'
    Risk factor assessments
    Counselling
    Individual educational materials

B. *Focus on groups*
    I Didactic group methods
       Lecture–discussion
       Seminars
       Conference
    II Experiential group methods
       Skills training
       Behaviour modification
       Sensitivity/Encounter
       Inquiry learning
       Peer group discussion
       Simulation
       Role play
       Self-help

C. *Focus on populations*
    I Social marketing and the media
    II Community organisation and community development
    III Environmental adaptations

Source: Egger, Spark & Lawson 1990.

Structure of the book

THE BOOK IS divided into two main parts. Part 1 deals with principles of media use, and Part 2 discusses their applications. In Part 1, Chapter 1, we look at the historical development of mass media in health promotion; evidence relevant to the effectiveness of using mass media; and broad issues with respect to the influence of the mass media on beliefs, attitudes and behaviour in general. Chapter 2 explains basic communication principles relevant to media use and presents a communication model used as a basis for many of the practical applications set out in Part 2. Finally, a social marketing approach to health is considered in Chapter 3, concluding with a structure for the applied processes examined in Part 2.

In Part 2, we consider the five Ms of the communication program: *medium, market, message, method* and *measures*. The background and framework for this classification is covered in Chapter 4. Each of the following five chapters then covers one of the Ms. Chapter 5 considers the media and presents a range of mass media from mass reach media such as network television and metropolitan newspapers, to more limited reach media such as posters and brochures. Chapter 6 discusses the market in terms of market segmentation and describes two models of audience segmentation. Chapters 7 and 8 consider the development of media messages and Chapters 9–11 cover major methods of presentation (i.e. advertising, publicity, edutainment). Chapter 12 considers the measures used both for developing and evaluating media campaigns. Finally, Chapter 13 presents a summary of guidelines for implementing successful mass media campaigns.

Many of the campaigns referred to throughout this book have been developed by the authors themselves over the years. This is not meant to imply that these are in any way better than any other campaigns in which the authors were not involved, but merely indicates a greater familiarity with our own materials. We have also attempted to use as examples only those campaigns or materials that have been the subject of some form of evaluation. In doing so, we are aware that we may have missed some major media programs. We also make no excuses for the sometimes heavy emphasis on quit smoking media initiatives, because that is the area of complex behaviour change in which there has been a large number of interventions and most success in recent times.

Definition of terms

The following are definitions of some of the terms used in this book:

Advertising: the paid placement of messages in the media by an identified source, usually with the aim of creating, changing or maintaining some attitude toward the source or toward the content of the message.

Advocacy: use of the media in a variety of ways, both paid and unpaid (but mostly unpaid), to influence the public agenda, usually on a controversial issue.

Campaign or program: a planned set of activities designed to achieve a defined set of objectives.

Community development: the process of achieving health promotion goals through empowering the community to identify its health needs and to assume responsibility for planning, controlling and evaluating progress to meet these needs.

Community organisation (sometimes called social mobilisation): the bringing together of intersectoral allies to raise awareness of, and demand for, a particular program, to assist in the delivery of resources and services and to strengthen community participation and ownership (McKee 1992).

Edutainment: the deliberate placement of messages in entertainment media to achieve some social or educational objectives.

Mass media: the means of communication that reach large numbers of people. Sometimes referred to simply as 'the media'.

Media vehicle: a specific program (electronic) or publication (print) within a medium—for example, the 7.30 pm news on television, *Women's Weekly* magazine.

Method: a tactic employed as part of a strategy. Methods describe the means by which change is to be brought about within the target group.

Public relations: the combination of processes (including publicity) used to create and maintain favourable attitudes towards an organisation or cause.

Publicity: unpaid use of the media to place specific messages before the public, usually via news and current affairs programs.

Social marketing: the design, implementation and control of programs aimed at increasing the acceptability of a social idea or practice in one or more groups of target adopters (Kotler 1972).

Strategy (in health promotion): a plan of action that anticipates resources for achieving specific objectives and possible barriers in doing this (Green, Kreuter, Deeds & Partridge 1980).

PART 1

Principles

'Selling' health through the media is not new

1

Background to the use of the media in health promotion

Don't trust what you read in health and diet books. You might die of a misprint. (Mark Twain)

*T*RADITIONALLY, HEALTH information was passed on in a clinical or one-to-one setting—doctor to patient, mother to child. As populations grew and communication technologies improved, mass media became available—and necessary—to supply health information to individuals. Initially, this was in the form of 'limited-reach' print media such as brochures, pamphlets, posters and small circulation newsheets. The 1940s and 1950s saw a larger-scale use of mass media for public 'information' campaigns. These dealt with topics such as hygiene and immunisation in a manner which can best be described as health 'education'. Since then, the advent of sophisticated electronic media and a better understanding of communication processes has led to the development of campaigns that not only provide health information, but also attempt to persuade individuals to adopt recommended healthy behaviours. Even more recently, the media have become a vehicle for advocacy of social, political and legislative change in modern societies.

Electronic media (television in particular) made possible 'broadcasting' or communication to 'broad' groups and categories of people. While this was seen as a boost to educational opportunities, hindsight shows that it was the lack of a sophisticated targeting approach which explains the failure of many early campaigns and the consequent pessimism about media use for public education which pervaded the literature at the time (Hyman & Sheatsley 1947; Bauer 1964). A predominant belief was that the public were resistant to media messages because of apathy, attitudinal defensiveness and an inability to process complex information.

A diametrically opposing view, often accepted by the less analytical, was that the media could be used at will to sway the population to particularly 'righteous' points of view that would seem to be of obvious benefit to the individual. This simplistic approach was known as the 'injection' or 'hypodermic needle' approach to education (Atkin 1981), which Rogers and Shoemaker (1971) defined as the process by which messages are transferred through certain channels from a source to a receiver. The failure of the 'hypodermic needle' approach was most notable in areas of complex behaviour change such as modification of sexual behaviour and drug use. The shift away from this approach began in the 1950s with the so-called Elmira and Decatur studies (Klapper 1961) which set out to answer not whether the mass media can or do have an effect, but rather under what conditions they have effects.

A more rational view is now developing from an emerging analytical and theoretical literature encompassing all aspects of education, persuasion and influence (see Atkin 1985). This suggests that the mass media *can* be used successfully in promoting health *under certain circumstances*. As we made clear in discussing selection of strategies for health promotion, the three words best defining the limitations are '. . . it all depends' (Egger, Spark & Lawson 1990). It has been the aim of much recent research to understand and detail the circumstances defining which media and media messages are effective as well as the circumstances under which various aspects of health can be influenced. Some of these conditions are summarised at the end of this chapter.

The media as a source of health information

ONE IMPETUS FOR using the mass media to promote health has come from their apparent effectiveness in promoting products such as tobacco, alcohol and non-nutritious foods that are associated with ill-health. Studies of commercial media use in these areas have suggested that approaches other than simple information transmission can be effective—for example, the role of publicity and sponsorship in smoking promotions (Chapman & Egger 1980; Aitkin et al. 1987), tapping consumer motivations in food advertising (Rubinstein 1987) and targeting of messages in alcohol advertising (Bevins 1988).

Cigarette advertising, in particular, has become extremely skilful over the years because of the vast funds available and the need to circumvent increasing restrictions on advertising. At the same time, health professionals have attempted to understand the psychological processes involved in advertising campaigns aimed at young smokers and to use these in developing anti-smoking media promotions (see Chapman & Egger 1983). A large number of anti-smoking campaigns have been developed in recent times, many of which have incorporated some of these principles (for a critical review of these campaigns, see Flay 1987).

Young Man in White

You may call him an "interne," but in name and in fact he's every inch a doctor.

He has his textbook education...his doctor's degree. But, in return for the privilege of working side by side with the masters of his profession, he will spend a year—more likely two—as an active member of a hospital staff.

His hours are long and arduous...his duties exacting. But when he finally hangs out his coveted shingle in private practice he will be *a doctor with experience!*

According to a recent Nationwide survey:

MORE DOCTORS SMOKE CAMELS THAN ANY OTHER CIGARETTE

YOUR "T-ZONE" WILL TELL YOU...

T for Taste...
T for Throat...
that's your proving ground for any cigarette. See if Camels don't suit your "T-Zone" to a "T."

R. J. Reynolds Tobacco Company. Winston-Salem, N. C.

❧ The makers of Camels take an understandable pride in the results of a nationwide survey among 113,597 doctors by three leading independent research organizations.

When queried about the cigarette they themselves smoked, the brand named most by the doctors was...Camel.

And these doctors represented every branch of medicine—general physicians, surgeons, diagnosticians, and specialists.

Like you, doctors smoke for pleasure. The rich, full flavor and cool mildness of Camel's superb blend of costlier tobaccos are just as appealing to them as to you.

CAMELS *Costlier Tobaccos*

The changing times: with cigarette advertising now banned in Australia, this ad promoting smoking for health reasons appears particularly incongruous

A second impetus for using mass media in health promotion comes from surveys which show that the media are a major source of health information for the general public (National Institute of Mental Health 1982; Macro Systems 1987). However, content analyses show that health issues are often incompletely or incorrectly dealt with in mass media (e.g. Amos 1986; Wallack & Dorfman 1992). Hence, health professionals should not only take the opportunity provided by the media, but should also attempt to ensure that health information provided by non-health sources is accurate. While developing specific health messages in health authority advertisements may be relatively straightforward, attempting to ensure that news and entertainment vehicles deal responsibly with health issues is far more complex. These issues will be addressed in later chapters.

Effectiveness of mass media community trials to promote health

IN THE 1970S, several large-scale community health promotion trials involving the mass media were carried out in a number of countries around the world. Three of the best known of these were the Stanford three (and later five) city studies in the United States (Maccoby et al. 1977), the North Karelia project in Finland (Puska et al. 1985, 1985a) and the North Coast Healthy Lifestyle Program in Australia (Egger et al. 1983). These studies generally involved comparing the impact of mass-media-only interventions versus mass-media-plus-community programs with control communities having no interventions. The general conclusion from these studies is that maximum change is best achieved through the combination of mass media and community-based programs, and that mass media alone may also have an impact.

The effectiveness of the media, either alone or as a contributing element in health promotion campaigns, has been confirmed in a number of different areas (e.g. see Flay 1987; Atkin 1979), although some reviewers have pointed out the equivocal nature of much of the evidence (e.g. Redman, Spencer & Sanson-Fisher 1990; Vingilis & Coultes 1990; McGuire 1986). Nevertheless, even these reviewers concede that many interventions have not been fair tests of the potential effectiveness of mass media because of factors such as insufficient media weight (i.e. insufficient message exposure), poor message development, inadequate message targeting, a lack of skills and expertise in using the media, and even a difficulty in evaluating the full effectiveness of such programs. However, where mass media campaigns have been based on sound communication principles and have been developed with close co-operation between health and media professionals, they have had substantial impact (e.g. France et al. 1991).

Much of the discrepancy in the results of large-scale media campaigns has been due to differences in quality and weight of media presence. Furthermore, many early United States attempts to use the media lacked professional input. For example, in the

---

'The media don't work: the great health media debate

The mass media are so *pervasive* and the source of so much of the information we have about the world, including health knowledge, that it's difficult to avoid the conclusion that the mass media are also a *persuasive* influence on our lives. However, reviews of research evidence usually conclude that the effects obtained are either: (1) relatively small (e.g. McGuire 1986; Cook, Kendierski & Thomas 1983); (2) inconclusive (e.g. Freedman 1984); or (3) contingent upon various conditions that limit the ability to make generalisations based on the results (Roberts & Maccoby 1985).

On the other hand, the public and various lobby groups vociferously express the view that the media do affect us, particularly in areas such as: violence; pornography; unfair stereotyping of the aged, women and ethnic groups; advertising to children; the advertising of alcohol and tobacco products.

In the meantime, commercial organisations continue to spend large sums of money on advertising and publicity to achieve sales and other goals. They obviously believe that media have an impact, and one that is measurable. Furthermore, studies of specific, well-designed and well-implemented mass media campaigns show that the media can have a substantial impact in both the health area (e.g. France et al. 1991; Flay 1987), and in other social areas (e.g. Donovan & Leivers 1993; Coleman & Meyer 1990).

United States it is federal government policy not to allow the Department of Health and Human Services to use paid advertising for health promotion (although some health professionals have strongly argued for this policy to be reversed, particularly since the advent of AIDS (e.g. see Warner 1987)). Campaigns such as the Centres for Disease Control's National AIDS Information and Education campaign, although using professional media agencies for message development, have had to rely on voluntary placement of public service announcements for their main media exposure. This has resulted in low exposure and a less than optimal impact of the campaign (Donovan et al. 1991).

In Australia, on the other hand, commercial advertising ideas and personnel have been involved in paid advertising campaigns since the 1960s. In some of these early efforts there was perhaps too much responsibility given to media professionals because health professionals lacked expertise and confidence in dealing with the media. More recently, a greater balance has been achieved and this balance needs to be sustained to prevent any naive approaches to paid advertising for health promotion which can come from either side. Techniques for achieving this are covered in Chapter 9.

The 'Life. Be In It' campaign, which commenced in the mid 1970s, was the first large-scale national media campaign in Australia aimed at influencing health-related behaviour (i.e. physical activity). As such, it suffered the disadvantage of no formal evaluation and no clear indications of expected outcome. It was also based on unreal expectations of media influence characterised by the 'hypodermic needle' approach discussed above. Other smaller-scale campaigns targeted at smoking were pioneered by the Victorian Anti-Cancer Council, the National Heart Foundation, the Health Department of Western Australia and the NSW Health Department. These, and later larger-scale campaigns, no doubt had a significant effect in creating an atmosphere for advocacy of health, particularly in issues such as smoking, which has developed since the 1970s.

The 'North Coast Healthy Lifestyle Program', which began on the North Coast of NSW in 1978, was one of the first major controlled studies of mass media influences in health promotion in Australia. This followed similar approaches in the United States and Finland, and demonstrated that smoking prevalence could be significantly reduced on a population basis through a mass-mediated campaign incorporating social marketing, paid advertising and community organisation techniques (Egger et al. 1983). The early to mid-eighties saw a number of statewide campaigns directed at smoking and drink driving, and the launch of national campaigns against AIDS and drug abuse.

These earlier experimental media health campaigns were invaluable for the insight they provided into the benefits of the 'advertising' approach to promote health. On a wider scale they also increased health professionals' knowledge and awareness of the value of social marketing—the adoption of marketing principles in areas deemed to be for the social good. From these earlier campaigns came also an increased understanding of the ways in which media could be used for public relations and publicity at low, or no cost to the initiator, both to promote health at the individual level and to advocate changes conducive to health at the social, economic, organisational and political levels.

The roles of media in health promotion in recent times have become those of informing (educating) and motivating (persuading) at the individual level (i.e. developing personal skills) as well as advocating change at the social and political level (i.e. creating healthy environments). These roles are discussed in detail in Part 2. All have a place in health promotion, and each has advantages and disadvantages, depending on the circumstances. The issue, then, has become not one of determining whether media work, but under what circumstances and conditions they work best.

Components of successful media campaigns

A NUMBER OF researchers, both in health promotion and communication have attempted to identify the conditions under which media are most effective in promoting health. A detailed analysis of the components of successful and unsuccessful campaigns has been made by McGuire (1986), who concluded that the impact of media—even in studies that claim significant effects—may be only slight, but that the reasons for a null effect are often based on insufficient programming or analysis.

Douglas Solomon, who has been extensively involved in health media campaigns, including the Stanford Heart Disease Prevention Project, analysed good and bad media campaigns and concluded that campaigns that have been successful owe much of their success to:

1. the extensive use of formative research regarding audience and message variables

2. the supplementation of media with interpersonal communication within small groups that provide social support and modelling of appropriate behaviours (Solomon 1982; 1984)

Solomon proposes a framework for success consisting of four main factors:

1. *Adequate problem analysis* including the setting of detailed objectives (i.e. specific, measurable and reasonable), and audience segmentation.

2. *Appropriate media selection and use* including formative research to provide information about media-use patterns.

3. *Effective message design* determined by specific objective setting, the generation of alternative message approaches, pretesting and revision of campaign messages.

4. *Evaluation* including the study of both outcome and process evaluation.

The above attempts by McGuire (1986) and Solomon (1982; 1984) and a perusal of other research (Mendehlson 1973; National Institute of Health 1982; Rogers & Storey 1987; Elliot 1988) suggest a number of practical proposals for designing a successful campaign. These include the following:

1. *Carry out formative research.* Intuition is not sufficient for devising campaigns. Materials should be developed from skilled formative research (i.e. focus groups, surveys), pretested, and evaluated during exposure (see Chapter 12).

2. *Fully understand the topic being communicated.* Some topics are difficult and complex to teach (e.g. the nature of drugs and their effects), while others may be easily communicated (e.g. hygiene). Similarly, certain well-established behaviours are difficult to change (e.g. smoking), while others require only a minor effort (e.g. not littering).

3. *Use skilled creative personnel.* Determining a message is simple. Executing that message in a way that is optimally received and acted upon by a target audience is a highly skilled process (see Chapters 9–11).

4. *Understand the audience.* The extent to which a message is attended to, comprehended and used by an audience is largely determined by the extent to which the messenger understands the audience. Detailed profiles of an audience need to be established as a preliminary to media development if a message is to be optimally received (see Chapter 6).

5. *Target the message.* Different sub-groups have different needs, interests, beliefs and attitudes. Hence, different messages—or at least different message executions—should be tailored for different groups (see Chapter 7).

6. *Take account of interpersonal and peer influences.* Campaigns should attempt to stimulate interpersonal contact such as the promotion of group and community activities, and the activation of interpersonal communication networks (see Chapter 10).

7. *Maximise contact with the message.* This does not mean total bombardment. Research indicates that concentrated bursts of spot messages often work better

than the same quantity of messages strung out over a long period. Maximising contact also means optimising media within the constraints of a limited budget (see Chapter 5).

8. *Set a realistic duration for the study.* Many campaigns have not matched the duration of the study with the desired outcome. Longer campaigns are required to achieve behavioural change, whereas shorter campaigns may be sufficient for changes in awareness. Also, ongoing campaigns are necessary to maintain awareness and to reinforce attitude and behaviour change (see Chapter 13).

9. *Use multiple channels.* Multiple communication channels (i.e. different media and media vehicles plus various non-media channels) tend to have a synergistic effect, and can carry different types of information (see Chapter 4).

10. *Use a credible source or spokesperson.* Source credibility is a major factor affecting message acceptance. Spokespersons are selected on the assumption that they will be credible to the target audience. For example, the use of celebrities and sport stars in anti-drug promotions to youth is common practice. Yet research suggests that youth only identify with certain aspects of an idealised role model, such as his or her ability to play music or sport. If other aspects (e.g. his/her attitude to drugs) conflict with overwhelming peer pressure, the model will be discarded rather than the anti-social habit (see Chapter 8). Pretesting for credibility is essential in the message pretesting.

11. *Do not confuse logic and emotion.* A basic distinction can be drawn between rational and emotional messages in health. The former are less stimulating, better for intelligent audiences and are best represented in long copy print. The latter are motivational, better for attracting the interest of the indifferent, and best suited for the electronic media. In common parlance, the difference is between a message with 'light' versus a message with 'heat' (see Chapters 7 and 8).

12. *Set realistic goals.* Major shifts in behaviour are not common in large populations over short periods. Hence it is important that intermediate goals, for example, knowledge and attitudinal goals, are set rather than behavioural goals (see Chapter 3). Furthermore, many campaigns set large, unrealistic changes as their criteria for success (e.g. reducing alcoholism), rather than more realistic immediate changes (e.g. reducing the incidence of driving while drunk). Small changes (knowledge, attitudes and behaviour) in large groups are often more possible and can result in a greater degree of success throughout the population than can be achieved by large changes in small groups.

13. *Provide environmental supports for change.* Research has shown consistently that most media campaigns require 'on-the-ground' back-up support for optimum effect. To accomplish this, media should be accompanied by strategies associated with community organisation (see Chapter 13).

14. *Confirm that a mass media campaign is really justifiable.* Although listed last, whether a mass media campaign is both viable and justifiable should be

Findings concerning media use in health promotion

A precis of a number of research studies and implications for mass media use in the drug and alcohol area (Miller & Ware 1989) suggests that:

- Media may stimulate learning and generate often dramatic changes in behaviour where a level of pre-motivation exists. In many cases, however, mass media alone are insufficient for behaviour change and the mass media should be combined with personalised health education.
- The 'agenda setting' role of the media produces its most pervasive impact.
- In the short term, the influence of the mass media on its own tends to be in the direction of reinforcing existing beliefs and opinions and helping crystallise attitudes, rather than changing them.
- Mass media bestows 'prestige'; interpersonal communication bestows 'faith'; when both are combined, the chances of action are increased.
- Community development and interpersonal contact will be important components reinforcing, and being reinforced by, rigorously developed mass media messages and supporting printed materials.
- Through repetition, the mass media may produce long-term benefits by creating a climate of opinion or setting the agenda for public discussion.
- The simple persuasive model of mass media influences has now been replaced by a more socially oriented approach, in which the mass media are viewed as one of many possible sources of information in society. Mass media sources cannot be discussed in isolation from personal information sources—families, friends and so on—which may support or contradict their messages.
- The impact of a media message can no longer be determined by its content alone. Members of the audience are now regarded as active participants in the communication process and pre-existing beliefs, attitudes, experiences and knowledge affect attending to, interpretation and acceptance of messages.

determined early on, and presumably following the formative research phase. Mass media should be looked at in terms of costs and benefits and these should be compared with other strategies. If an alternative strategy is projected to be slightly less successful but at much less cost, the goals of a campaign may need to be re-examined. Often, a subsidiary aim of a campaign is to increase public awareness, or get more acceptance from funding bodies. In these cases a decision may still be taken to use the less cost-effective media approach (see Chapter 4).

Changes in public acceptance

Health promotion can have similarities to fashion design. Public acceptance is changeable and what may be acceptable (and effective) at one time may not be so at another. For example, in the 70s it was joked that a customer would ask a shopkeeper for a packet of cigarettes in a loud voice and a packet of condoms in a whisper. In the 90s, any self-respecting customer asks for condoms out loud and for cigarettes with a hand held over the mouth.

Summing up: when to use the media

IN CONCLUSION, IT is apparent that the media can be an effective tool in health promotion, given the appropriate circumstances and conditions. Some of the situations in which media have been found to be most appropriate are:

1. *When wide exposure is desired.* Mass media offer the widest possible exposure, although this may be at some cost. Cost-benefit considerations therefore are at the core of media selection.

2. *When the time frame is urgent.* Mass media offer the best opportunity for reaching either large numbers of people or specific target groups within a short time frame.

3. *When public discussion is likely to facilitate the educational process.* Media messages can be emotional and thought provoking. Because of the possible breadth of coverage, intrusion can occur at many different levels, stimulating discussion and thereby expanding the impact of a message.

4. *When awareness is a main goal.* By their very nature, the media are aware-ness-creating tools. Where awareness of a health issue is important to the resolution of that issue, the mass media can increase awareness quickly and effectively.

5. *When media authorities are 'on-side'.* Where journalists, editors and program-mers are 'on-side' with a particular health issue, this often guarantees greater support in terms of space and editorial content.

6. *When accompanying on-the-ground back-up can be provided.* Regardless of whether media alone are sufficient to influence health behaviour, it is clear that the success of media is improved with the support of back-up programs and services.

7. *When long-term follow-up is possible.* Most health behaviour changes require constant reinforcement. Media programs are most effective where the opportu-nity exists for long-term follow-up. This can take the form of short bursts of media activity over an extended period, or follow-up activities unrelated to media.

8. *When a generous budget exists.* Paid advertising, especially via television, can be very expensive. Even limited reach media such as pamphlets and posters can be expensive, depending on quality and quantity. For media to be consid-ered as a strategy in health promotion, careful consideration of costs and benefits needs to be undertaken.

9. *When the behavioural goal is simple.* Although complex behaviour change such as smoking cessation or exercise adoption may be initiated through media programs, the nature of media is such that simple behaviour changes such as immunisation or cholesterol testing are more easily stimulated through the media. In general, the more complex the behaviour change, the more non-media back-up is required to supplement a media health program.

10. *When the 'agenda' includes public relations.* Whether we acknowledge it or not, many, if not most health promotion programs have an 'agenda' which is not always explicit. Such an agenda may be to gain public support or acknowledgment, to solicit political favour or to get funds for further programs. Where public relations are either an explicit or implicit goal of a program, mass media are effective because of their wide-ranging exposure.

2

Principles of communication relevant to media use

*We are coming to recognise that there is a marketplace
of ideas just as there is a marketplace of goods.* (Kotler 1984)

E VERY DAY in a modern society, individuals are bombarded with 'messages'
or 'information'. Taken as a whole, this can be represented as 'clutter':

clutterclutterclutterclutterclutterclutterclutterclutterclutter
clutterclutterclutterclutterclutterclutterclutterclutterclutter
clutterclutterclutterclutterclutterclutterclutterclutterclutter
clutterclutterclutterclutterclutterclutterclutterclutterclutter
clutterclutterclutterclutterclutterclutterclutterclutterclutter
clutterclutterclamourclutterclutterclutterclutterclutterclutter
clutterclutterclutterclutterclutterclutterclutterclutterclutter
clutterclutterclutterclutterclutterclutterclutter

Any message health professionals wish to communicate is hidden in this clutter
(like the single word 'clamour' in the lower left-hand side of the picture). It should,
therefore, be our objective to make this message stand out more clearly, not only
through mechanical processes of execution, such as intensity, frequency or size of the
message (i.e. 'clamour' would stand out from the clutter if it was in a larger and bolder
typeface), but also through a knowledge of individual psychological factors such as
selective attention (see below).

In contrast to the 'hypodermic needle' approach to communication, today's communication experts emphasise the fact that the receiver is an *active* integrator of

information, not simply a passive receiver. Hence, rather than the message acting on the receiver, the receiver acts on the message. In relation to advertising this has been expressed as '. . . ask not what your advertising does to the consumer, but what the consumer does to your advertising'.

Active information processing

THE MAJOR FEATURE of active information processing is that it is selective. This selectivity operates in three ways:

1. selective exposure (or attention)
2. selective perception
3. selective retention

Basically, this implies:

- that people expose themselves or pay attention to messages that have a personal relevance to them, or with which they already agree
- that when they are exposed to information that is not in agreement with their attitudes, individuals tend to reinterpret this information so that it is in accord with their existing attitudes and beliefs
- that even if the information that is not in agreement with their attitudes is committed to memory, it is often recalled in a light that is more favourable towards pre-existing attitudes and beliefs

1. Selective attention

It is physically impossible for any individual to respond to all incoming stimulation or information (Ornstein 1986). Instead, individuals selectively attend to stimuli, screening out much information in the process. This means that a considerable amount of exposure is deliberate (or voluntary), and hence efforts need to be made to enhance the likelihood of attention being given to any intended messages.

For example, a number of studies have shown that voters are more likely to expose themselves to messages from the political parties to which they are already committed (Klapper 1961). Similarly, smokers, especially those who find it difficult to quit or who want to keep on smoking, tend to avoid anti-smoking messages but pay attention to news or other reports that question or contradict the relationship between smoking and ill-health.

2. Selective perception and interpretation

Even if individuals do expose themselves to a message, they may not accept that message because of the processes of selective perception and interpretation. For example, following the surprising popularity of the 'All In The Family' show (a United States version of the British show . . . 'Til Death Us Do Part'), which features a right-wing 'conservative' older-generation couple generally in conflict with a younger-

> ## The changing face of fact
>
> Science, like art, can often be caught red-faced. It's vital, therefore, for health professionals working in the media to have a solid grounding in the scientific facts surrounding an issue. The ads shown here attempt to convince women, against common knowledge to the contrary, that they won't put on weight after quitting smoking. After these ads were made, scientific research confirmed that most ex-smokers *do* put on weight unless they take deliberate steps to avoid doing so.
>
>

generation 'liberal left-wing' couple, surveys found that the show appealed both to those with left-wing views *and* those with right-wing views. Although the show was meant to be satirical of right-wing prejudices, left-wingers as well as right-wingers saw it as endorsing their respective views (Vidmar & Rokeach 1974).

The selective interpretation of messages results, for example, in smokers questioning the scientific validity of data linking smoking to ill-health or rejecting the generalisation of these findings to themselves. Inconclusive data are particularly vulnerable to selective interpretation or what is called 'biased assimilation'. Lord, Ross and Lepper (1979) found that when pro and anti capital punishment groups were presented with studies showing mixed results on the deterrent effects of capital punishment, each interpreted the results as supportive of its own position. Hence health messages in the media cannot afford to be accompanied by the types of qualifications usually found in academic scientific reports.

3. Selective retention

In some cases of distortion it is difficult to determine whether incoming information is distorted at the perception stage or after it is stored in the memory. However, there is some evidence that 'memory' is sometimes 'reconstructed' in line with attitudes and expectations, rather than being the retrieval of inaccurately stored information. In a classic study, Allport and Postman (cited in Klapper 1961) showed subjects a picture of a confrontation in a train between a white man holding a razor and a black man. Subjects were asked to describe the picture to others, who in turn, were to describe it to others. As the story progressed, the razor shifted from the white man to the black man's hand, illustrating the influence of prejudice on retention.

Factors influencing the selectivity process

THREE MAJOR SETS of factors influence whether or not messages are attended to:

1. mechanical factors (e.g. intensity, sensational headlines, contrast with surrounding content)
2. psychological factors (e.g. personal interest, prior experiences)
3. message execution tactics (e.g. two-sided versus one-sided messages)

1. Mechanical factors

Mechanical factors are particularly important when messages must compete for attention against a large number of other messages or against a strong background. For example:

- eye-catching pictures greatly increase readership of print articles
- colour stands out in predominantly black and white productions
- larger ads attract more attention than smaller ads
- movement gains reflexive attention (e.g. flashing lights, moving arrows)
- isolated stimuli (e.g. lots of white space around a brief message in a newspaper ad) attract greater attention, as do objects placed in the centre, rather than on the periphery of the visual field

Given that the vast majority of smokers never notice health warnings on cigarette packs and in ads (FTC News Summary 1981; Fischer et al. 1989), studies in Australia have resulted in space, position and typeface size requirements to enhance the noticeability of cigarette pack health warnings (Centre for Behavioural Research in Cancer 1992).

2. Psychological factors

Psychological factors relate to the individual's self-interest and current *attitudes* and *beliefs*. People are more willing to respond to messages relating to topics of personal interest or messages that offer a personal benefit, and, for 'high involvement' issues, to messages that are consistent with what they already believe. Expectations also affect interpretation (i.e. people interpret information so that it is consistent with what they expect) and individuals also differ in their ability to attend to and process information.

A *belief* can be defined as a perception that a certain state of affairs exists or is true. An *attitude* can be defined as the extent to which positive or negative feelings are held toward a state of affairs. A 'state of affairs' can include objects, persons, behaviours or ideas. The *salience* of a belief refers to the readiness with which that belief 'comes to mind' when the person's attention is drawn to the issue.

Most attitudes are based on a set of beliefs and an evaluation of these beliefs. Some beliefs may be negative while others are positive. For attitudes where there is a mix of both negative and positive beliefs (as in many health and related policy areas), research suggests that the overall attitude held at a particular time depends on the

---

Personalising the message

According to Bevins (1987), much of the fault with public communications is that its central orientation is

WE

Health professionals often start from the incorrect assumption that WE know what THEY want to hear. In Bevin's terms, health authorities too often '. . . go around *"we-ing"* in public' when they should be personalising the message—that is, focusing on the mirror inversion of WE

ME

According to Bevins (1988):

> *Message begins with 'me'. Me singular. Indeed, there is no such thing really as mass communication. It's a contradiction in terms. Communication is an intensely personal, one-to-one process, whether you're doing it over the telephone or over the television network. Uni, Uno, One—is the very heart of communication.*

---

relative salience of the various positive and negative beliefs. Hence situations that stimulate consciousness of positive beliefs about an issue will increase the likelihood of an individual expressing a positive attitude toward that issue at that time. Conversely, negative attitudes will be produced if consciousness of negative beliefs is stimulated. If the aim is to achieve a change in attitude towards a particular issue, the message strategy should first stimulate recall of beliefs favourable to the issue prior to the persuasive component of the message being presented. For example, a target audience may believe that exercise is beneficial to overall health, tones the body and increases energy, but lacks sufficient motivation to participate. The persuasive message strategy might be that exercise can be fun, can increase alertness and is socially rewarding. However, before presenting these messages, the audience should be reminded of their positive beliefs.

It is also important to recognise that many members of a target audience may be ambivalent about an issue. For example, a woman may believe that condoms are a reliable, inexpensive, easy-to-use method for avoiding contracting a sexually transmitted disease. At the same time, she may also believe that condoms reduce pleasurable feelings for her partner, are embarrassing to purchase and present, and are difficult to dispose of afterwards.

The general message strategy therefore should be to:

1. reinforce and avoid alienating those who hold predominantly positive beliefs

2. create positive beliefs amongst those who are neutral towards the concept
3. neutralise and avoid intensifying currently held negative beliefs; and, in doing the above
4. ensure that all relevant beliefs are considered, that is, not just those specific to the behaviour, issue or object, but also the implications and consequences stemming from these

3. Message factors

Message execution tactics, including the language, tone and style of a message, are important influences on the impact of a communication. Tactics that increase message acceptance in high-involvement controversial areas include the following:

- linking the desired belief to an already accepted belief (e.g. most smokers accept that tobacco smoke constituents 'can't be doing you any good')
- staying within the target audience's 'latitude of acceptance' (i.e. the claimed threat and/or promised benefit must be credible)
- using two-sided messages rather than one-sided messages (i.e. accept that smoking can be enjoyable, help cope with stress, and act as a social facilitator)
- leaving the audience to draw their own conclusions rather than 'telling' them to adopt the promoted stance. Successful quit smoking advertisements are those that are seen by smokers *not* to be 'preaching' or 'dictating' to them

The processes of selective attention and processing are illustrated in Figure 2.1.

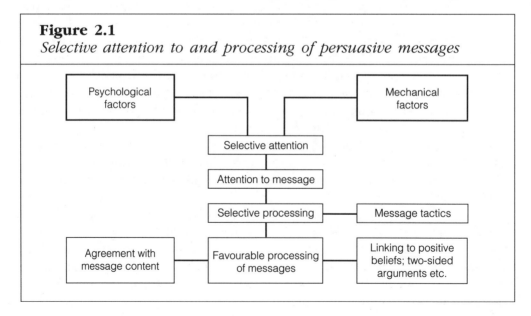

Figure 2.1
Selective attention to and processing of persuasive messages

Implications for initiating the communication process

WHEN IMPLEMENTING A communication (or persuasion) campaign to create awareness of and positive attitudes towards a concept, the first step of the campaign should focus on issues where there is most agreement between the target audience's attitudes and beliefs and those of the campaign source. This is because people are most receptive to, and accepting of, attitudes and beliefs they already hold. In many cases, these areas of agreement may have low salience (i.e. are rarely thought about), or are not strongly held. Exposure increases the salience of these attitudes and beliefs, and, depending on the persuasive power of the message, can also increase the strength of the attitudes and beliefs.

Approaching the communication process from a point of common agreement also builds source credibility and trust, and hence some form of commitment to the source and the message. This approach provides a favourable context within which to neutralise negative attitudes and beliefs, and to create positive attitudes and beliefs from a neutral position.

Once this platform of credibility is established, strategies such as attaching a negative belief to a positive belief to increase the likelihood of acceptance of the negative belief can be implemented.

A further executional tactic in implementing a communication campaign is to pre-empt potential counter-arguments that might otherwise distract from the message and/or lead to denigration of source credibility and hence rejection of the message.

The following guidelines, based on an understanding of the processes of communication, are useful for developing communication campaigns:

1. Establish source credibility by seeking a common point of agreement from which to commence the communication process.
2. Increase the salience and intensity of already held positive beliefs and of other beliefs that provide a positive context within which to change negative beliefs.
3. Link messages towards which people have potentially negative responses to already-held positive beliefs.
4. Avoid broaching issues that generate negative responses until prior positive beliefs are firmly established.
5. Attempt changes in negative beliefs slowly and in small steps, that is, stay within the target audience's 'latitude of acceptance' and do not make extreme claims.
6. Enhance source credibility by presenting apparently even-handed or two-sided approaches that pre-empt counter-arguments that would otherwise distract from the message or lead to its rejection.

A practical model for media use

MODELS FOR MEDIA use usually include two components:

1. a system overview showing the major variables in the media process
2. an effects component showing the expected outcomes in sequence.

Early communication models focused primarily on one or the other, or on much simplified combinations. For example, the 'hypodermic' approach used a simple systems model such as:

SOURCE → CHANNEL → RECEIVER

and a simple hierarchy of effects model such as:

KNOWLEDGE → ATTITUDE CHANGE → BEHAVIOUR

That is, information would be 'automatically' accepted, would lead to a change in attitude and would produce the desired behaviour change.

The 'spiral of silence'

The 'spiral of silence' phenomenon (Noelle-Neumann 1974) has been put forward as a way of explaining how the 'bandwagon effect' can develop. It suggests that as people see a different opinion from their own appear to grow in popularity (even if their view is the majority view), they become less inclined to express their own opinion in public. As this unwillingness spreads, and because the alternative opinion continues to be publicly expressed, this differing opinion appears to become even more popular. Fear of public isolation may even lead people to change their opinion so that it is in line with what they consider will be the *future* majority opinion.

The 'spiral of silence' concept is based on the proposition that an individual's beliefs and attitudes result from an interaction with the social environment, and that the perception of social opinions can have a major impact on the formation, change and expression of beliefs and attitudes. From a practical point of view, the important concepts are that individuals can be influenced by (a) what they perceive to be the majority view, and (b) which view they believe to be gaining most in strength. Views that are gaining in strength tend to have most impact.

The quit smoking movement has used the spiral of silence by activating the voice of the previously silent majority of non-smokers. The quit smoking lobby, via a sustained, carefully planned and implemented media publicity campaign reinforced by 'Quit' advertising, has created the perception that anti-smoking attitudes are gaining in strength and are the 'opinion of the future.'

However, the inadequacy of this approach is clearly evident, particularly in relation to a health behaviour such as cigarette smoking (Flay 1987), and where attitude change can follow, or be unrelated to, behaviour change (Zimbardo et al. 1977). As Wallack (1985) concluded, the results of past mass media efforts to change behaviour clearly show that such efforts are more complicated than they appear.

The McGuire model

There have been many models of the communication process. McGuire (1985) has presented a comprehensive approach where the system overview consists of *input factors* and the effects consist of *output factors*. The input factors may be viewed as independent variables and the consequent effects as dependent variables.

Input factors are those variables that tend to be under the control of, or selected by, the sender of the message, whereas *output factors* are those effects that take place in the target audience. McGuire's input variables are a formalised statement of Lasswell's (1948) original statement of communication as ' . . . who says what, by what medium, to whom and directed at what sort of behaviour'. These are termed respectively: *source, message, channel, receiver,* and *destination.*

Source factors refer to the perceived characteristics of the organisation or person sending the message. Factors such as credibility, gender, ethnicity and attractiveness have been studied in terms of the relative impact of the message as a function of these perceived characteristics of the source.

Message factors refer to the type of appeal, style and tone of the message, and a whole host of variables studied in social psychology (e.g. one-sided versus two-sided messages; warm versus cool messages (Klapper 1961)).

Channel factors refer to the form and impact of the medium through which the message is transmitted. For example, different media (i.e. verbal, visual, electronic versus print media) are suitable for different sorts of messages, and different media vehicles also may have differential credibility (e.g. the *Australian* versus the *Truth* newspapers).

The knowledge–attitude–behaviour conundrum

The association between knowledge, attitudes and behaviour is a complicated one that has long been misunderstood, particularly in the field of drug education (Miller & Ware 1989). It has been assumed, for example, that informing people about the dangers of drugs will help in the prevention or reduction of problematic drug use. However, often this is known not to be the case. In fact, drug users frequently—but not always—are more knowledgeable about drug use than non-users (Mendehlson 1973).

Also, there is no consistent association between attitudes and behaviour change. It is typically thought that changing attitudes will lead to behaviour change, but sometimes attitude change *follows* rather than *precedes* behaviour change. Examples of this are the compulsory wearing of seat belts and bicycle helmets and drink-driving restrictions. Attitudes towards these behaviours tend to become more positive after people (are required to) carry out the behaviours. This has meant that greater emphasis has been placed on legislation rather than on education for prevention, particularly in many areas of injury prevention.

eceiver factors refer to characteristics of the audience, including both demographic nd lifestyle variables and, of particular importance, pre-existing attitudes and beliefs with respect to the message.

Destination factors are variables related to the types of behaviour targeted by the campaign (e.g. one-off behaviours such as immunisation, HIV testing or mammograph testing as opposed to sustained lifestyle changes such as quitting smoking or adopting an exercise program). They are also variables related to the successive sub-steps required for the communication to be effective. For example, the target audience must first be exposed to the message. Having been exposed, it must attend to the message, become interested in it, understand it, agree with or accept the message, store the content in memory, retrieve the information from memory at the appropriate time, and then adopt or try to adopt and maintain the behaviour.

McGuire has presented his model as the input/output matrix shown in Table 2.1.

Table 2.1
McGuire's communication/persuasion model

Output-Persuasion Variables	Input-Communication Variables				
	Source	Message	Channel	Receiver	Destination
Exposure					
Interest					
Comprehension					
Skill acquisition					
Attitude change					
Memory storage					
Information retrieval					
Decision making					
Behaviour					
Reinforcement					
Consolidation					

Source: McGuire 1986.

The Rossiter model

Following McGuire, Rossiter and his colleagues (Rossiter & Percy 1987; Rossiter, Percy & Donovan 1984) have developed a simplified six-step model relating advertising exposure to company objectives and profits. However, the model is applicable to all forms of media use (see Donovan & Owen 1993). The six steps are shown on the left-hand side of Table 2.2. Examples of the types of activities or measures appropriate to each step are shown on the right-hand side of Table 2.2.

Table 2.2
The six-step communication process

Step	Examples
1. Exposure	Media advertising and publicity, seminars, videos
2. Message processing (short-term memory)	Attention, learning, acceptance, emotional arousal
3. Communication effects (long-term memory)	Knowledge, attitudes, intentions
4. Behavioural effects	Enquiry, visits to an 'outlet', attendance at seminars, trial, adoption
5. Sales/Market share	Population adoption rates, other measures of incidence and prevalence
6. Outcome goals	Reduced costs, profits/population outcome measures

Source: Rossiter, Percy & Donovan 1984.

Table 2.2 shows that the hierarchy of effects commences with exposure of the target audience to the message (Step 1). Messages may be exposed in TV ads, billboards, news items, posters, magazine articles, videos or face-to-face counselling.

Exposure and attention to the message lead to conscious processing of the message in short-term memory (Step 2). This involves attention to the message content, learning and comprehension, acceptance or rejection of the message, and emotional arousal.

Processing of the message results in long-term memory effects called 'communication effects' (Step 3). These are beliefs about, attitudes towards, and intentions with respect to the message topic and promoted behaviour (for example, health and fitness, immunisation). The content of the message, the audience's initial attitudes and beliefs, the nature of the message exposure and the degree of repetition of the message all affect what is stored in long-term memory and how easily it can be recalled later.

The desired communication effects, when recalled during decision making should, all other things being equal, facilitate behavioural effects such as making further enquiries, or other intermediate behavioural effects, or actual trial of the recommended behaviour (Step 4). For example, a smoker may call a 'Quit' help line, a teenager may send for more information about STDs, or a woman may talk to her GP about the pros and cons of having a mammogram. On the other hand, the campaign objective might be reinforcing behaviours that already exist (e.g. feedback on reduced road crash figures).

These behavioural effects take place amongst pre-defined audiences that were the targets of the exposure schedule and message strategy. The accumulation of these behavioural effects amongst the target audience(s) leads to the achievement of the overall outcome objectives and goals—which in commercial terms are usually profit objectives, via sales and market share objectives (Steps 5 and 6). In the health area, 'sales' or 'market share' objectives may be stated in terms of participation rates or prevalence rates, while the overall goals relate to things like risk reductions, health cost reductions and/or more positive life experiences for the general population (Donovan & Owen 1993).

Implications for planning a communication strategy

IN PLANNING A communication strategy according to the Rossiter and Percy (1987) model discussed above, the chain is in the opposite direction to the exposure process. That is, the health promotion practitioner:

1. defines the overall outcome goals and specific measurable objectives; then
2. selects specific target audiences amongst whom to achieve these goals
3. specifies behavioural objectives required of each of the target audiences
4. delineates the beliefs and attitudes necessary to achieve the behavioural objectives
5. generates the content and types of messages that will be necessary to achieve these beliefs and attitudes
6. determines how, where and how often these messages are to be exposed or delivered to the specific target audiences

An example with respect to planning a health campaign aimed at reducing smoking is shown in Table 2.3.

Evaluating a communication strategy: setting realistic goals

DONOVAN AND ROBINSON (1992) argue that one reason many mass media campaigns are deemed 'failures' (Donohew 1990) or appear to have limited impact (McGuire 1986), is that they have been evaluated at a behavioural level rather than at preceding levels in the hierarchy of effects. For many campaigns, an evaluation at the behavioural level is simply inappropriate. Mass media are most effective in the early stages of the hierarchy (i.e. message delivery, awareness, knowledge and tentative attitude formation), whereas other elements of a campaign mix and environmental factors are far more influential at the later behavioural stages. For example, with respect to traffic safety, instead of directly setting numbers of road crashes and mortality/morbidity

Table 2.3
Steps in implementing a 'quit smoking' communication campaign using the Rossiter and Percy model (1987)

1. OUTCOME GOALS
   What overall goal do we want to achieve? Reduction of lung cancer, heart disease and other diseases related to smoking.

2. SPECIFIC OUTCOME OR IMPACT OBJECTIVES
   What measurable objectives do we need to reach to achieve this overall goal? For example, reduction of the number of smokers from 28% to 22% of the population by 1995.

3. TARGET AUDIENCE SELECTION AND BEHAVIOURAL OBJECTIVES
   What target audiences must we reach to achieve these objectives and what do we want them to do? Are there sub-groups of smokers that are more or less amenable to quit messages? How can they be described—demographically, years of smoking, amount smoked, gender, attitude towards quitting.

4. COMMUNICATION OBJECTIVES
   What beliefs and attitudes is it desirable for smokers to hold to induce them to try to quit? For example, smoking is harmful to health, quitting leads to a reduction in risk, quitting is possible, smoking is socially unacceptable, passive smoking affects loved ones.

5. PROCESSING OBJECTIVES
   What sorts of messages are needed to bring about appropriate processing so as to result in these beliefs and attitudes? For example, graphic reminders of harmful effects, Quit tips, fear arousal, testimonials. How will the message processing vary by target audience sub-group?

6. EXPOSURE/MEDIA OBJECTIVES
   How, where and how often do the messages need to be exposed to attract attention and to result in long-term belief and attitude changes? Mass media? Work-site promotions? Are different target audiences reached by different communication channels?

objectives, Mendehlson (1973) set middle-range goals, such as increasing awareness that most accidents result from subjective misconceptions of actual risks, and that alcohol directly affects the perception of risk. This resulted in measurable changes in attitudes to drinking and driving.

The evaluation of the effectiveness of a campaign depends not only on where in the hierarchy that effectiveness is measured, but also on how effective the campaign has been at each preceding level in the hierarchy. Figure 2.2 on p. 28 shows that the effectiveness of a campaign depends on the level in the hierarchy at which the campaign impact is measured. If we assume that 50% of the target audience is actually exposed to the message, 50% of these understand the message, and so on . . . we achieve a successful behavioural adoption of less than 1% of the target audience—a change hardly likely to be evident in standard campaign evaluations or even laboratory manipulations.

Communication as 'influence'

In his classic study of 'Influence', psychologist Robert Cialdini (1984) has identified a number of principles related to the psychology of persuasion which are relevant for all forms of communication.

1. ***Reciprocation*** implies that people try to repay, in kind, what another person has provided. The tactic explains the widespread use of 'free gifts' and 'product samples' in promotion.

2. ***Commitment*** leads to greater consistency between beliefs, attitudes and behaviour. Hence making a commitment (such as a bet on a horse race) has been shown to increase the better's confidence of the horse's chances of winning; signing a 'pledge' to lose weight increases the likelihood of successful weight control.

3. ***Social proof*** states that people look to the behaviour of others as a guide to what is appropriate or normative behaviour. It explains the use of canned laughter in comedy shows and, more seriously, the phenomena of 'copycat' suicides and violence.

4. ***Liking*** refers to the fact that people tend to like those who have similar attitudes, beliefs and backgrounds to their own. This is based on a perception of empathy with the other person. Hence spokespeople selected for endorsing a campaign or delivering a message should be seen by the target audience to have a sympathetic understanding of their position.

5. ***Authority*** relates to a deep-seated sense of duty many people have towards those in a respected position. For this reason the medical profession still wields enormous influence as the primary authority in the field of health.

6. ***Scarcity*** creates a desire among individuals for the scarce resource. This principle is used effectively in the 'limited stock only' type of promotion used regularly in advertising.

Figure 2.2

Potential effectiveness of a campaign given 50% success at each level DONOVAN & OWEN 1993

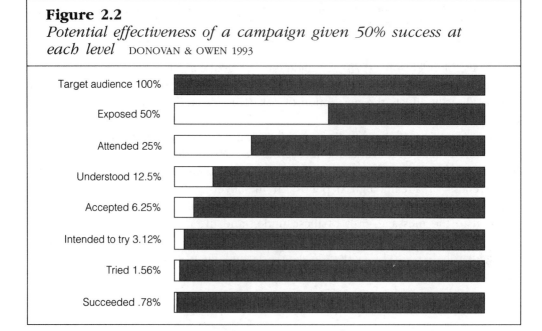

Target audience 100%	
Exposed 50%	
Attended 25%	
Understood 12.5%	
Accepted 6.25%	
Intended to try 3.12%	
Tried 1.56%	
Succeeded .78%	

Figure 2.2 also shows that even very successful efforts higher up the hierarchy need to be sustained to achieve any significant impact at the attitudinal and behavioural levels. It also is evident that failure at a higher level ensures failure at all lower levels. Hence, it is essential that campaigns be of sufficient duration and weight to achieve the desired change at the higher levels of this hierarchy. Many mass media health campaigns are simply too bland to attract attention, lack credibility and persuasiveness in their execution, do not have sufficient exposure, or are of too short a duration to achieve any sort of significant behaviour change.

3

Marketing health through the media

*The same disciplined, stepped approach that makes
marketing appeal to the commercial sector gives it appeal
amongst those who seek to change health behaviours.*

(Novelli 1984)

F OLLOWING A NUMBER of small-scale attempts in the 1960s—many in underdeveloped countries—the 1970s saw a substantial increase in the incorporation of marketing techniques into the planning and implementation of
campaigns designed to bring about social change (Fox & Kotler 1980; Manoff 1985).
A number of factors influenced this. One was the realisation by social scientists and
health professionals that, while they were expert in assessing what people should do,
they were not necessarily expert in communicating these messages, nor in motivating
or facilitating behavioural change. Another influence was the apparent success of
marketing techniques in the commercial area, and the observation that the discipline
of marketing provides a systematic, research-based approach for the planning and
implementation of mass-intervention programs. A third influence was the move in
public health towards the prevention of the so-called 'lifestyle' diseases such as heart
disease and cancer—an approach based on epidemiological research findings about
the relationships between habitual behaviours and long-term health outcomes (Wallack
1983).

In turn, this focus on lifestyle diseases led to an emphasis (some would say an
undue emphasis) on individual responsibility and behaviour change. Hence, there was
an increased acceptance of the marketing philosophy of individualism and rational free
choice. Some critics of social marketing have claimed that such a 'philosophy' largely
ignores the social, economic and environmental factors that influence individual health
behaviours. While some social marketing campaigns deserve this criticism, it shows a

lack of understanding of social marketing on both sides because one of the fundamental aspects of marketing—and hence of *social* marketing—is an awareness of the total environment in which the organisation operates, and how this environment influences, or can itself be influenced, to enhance the marketing activities of the company or health agency (Kotler 1988; Pride & Ferrell 1980).

The term 'social marketing' was first used by Kotler and Zaltman in 1971 to describe the application of the principles and methods of marketing to the achievement of socially desirable goals. Since then, there has been rapid growth in the use of marketing techniques in the health area in the United States, other industrialised nations and also in Third World countries. The 1980s saw a massive growth in mass media-based health promotion campaigns utilising marketing concepts, across a broad range of activities, including injury prevention, drinking and driving, seat belt usage, drugs, smoking, exercise, immunisation, nutrition, and heart disease prevention (Fine 1990; Kotler & Roberto 1989; Manoff 1985; Rice & Atkin 1989).

The increasing use of marketing practices by non-profit organisations and for social-change objectives, has led to a redefinition of the term 'marketing' from ' . . . the performance of business activities that direct the flow of goods and services from producer to consumer or user' (American Marketing Association 1960, page 15), to include the marketing of ideas, that is, ' . . . the process of planning and executing the conception, pricing, promotion, and distribution of ideas, goods, and services to create exchanges that satisfy individual and organisational objectives' (*Marketing News* 1985, page 1).

Social marketing defined

SOCIAL MARKETING IS now a clearly established subsection of marketing and is defined as ' . . . the design, implementation, and control of programs aimed at increasing the acceptability of a social idea or practice in one or more groups of target adopters' (Kotler & Roberto 1989, page 24).

Social marketing makes use of key concepts from mainstream product and service marketing: market segmentation; market research; competitive assessment; the use of product, price, promotion and distribution tactics; pretesting and ongoing evaluation of campaign strategies; and models of consumer behaviour adapted from psychological and communications literature.

For many health promotion professionals, social marketing is seen as synonymous with the use of mass media to promote socially desirable causes. This emphasis on the mass media is not unexpected, given that many social marketers see their basic product as information (Wallack 1983), or that they view social marketing as working primarily through channels of communication, with information as its primary resource (Young 1989). However, in commercial marketing, the use of mass media is only one component of the total marketing process. A product must also be designed to meet the buyers' 'needs': it must be packaged and priced appropriately; it must be easily

'Bread: it's a great way to go'

Sponsoring body: NSW Department of Health, local bakers.

Background: Elderly retired women have been found to have low fibre intakes and high rates of constipation. Formative research showed this might be increased by promoting (with bread producers) the advantages of eating more wholemeal and/or wholegrain bread.

Objectives:
1. Increase bread consumption in the elderly, and as a result
2. Decrease laxative use.

Media: Pamphlets, billboards.

Market: Retired couples (women in particular).

Message: Wholemeal/wholegrain bread consumption can decrease constipation.

Method: Advertising, publicity, community organisation.

Measures: Compared to a control town, sales of laxatives through pharmacies decreased by over 60% in the major test town, and this coincided with a 50% increase in bread sales.

Source: Egger et al. 1991.

accessible; it should be 'trial-able' (if a large commitment is required); intermediaries such as wholesalers and retailers must be established; and, where relevant, sales staff must be informed and trained. Only after all these factors are in place are the mass media used to make potential buyers:

- aware of the product
- aware of the product's benefits
- aware of where it may be purchased
- interested (i.e. motivated) to seek further information, or to purchase or trial the product

In the same way, a campaign that aims to promote health through encouraging individual behaviour change must be based on more than just mass media. Programs and strategies are required at community level, in such a manner that the activities promoted are: 'do-able' (i.e. within the target group's capacities); able to be tried out (to allow 'sampling' of an activity prior to long-term commitment of funds, effort or time); able to be learnt (i.e. skills must be defined and training must be available for specific activities); accessible and affordable. Social marketing, by definition, is a more comprehensive and effective approach than simply use of the media.

Principles and practices of social marketing

A NUMBER OF aspects of marketing have been discussed in the context of social marketing (e.g. Hastings & Haywood 1991; Kotler & Roberto 1989; Lancaster, McIlwain & Lancaster 1983; LeFebvre & Flora 1988; Manoff 1985; Novelli 1984; Solomon 1989). Those that are most relevant for health promotion, as summed up by Donovan and Owen (1993), are:

1. The marketing concept: a consumer orientation

'Marketing' is not only a discipline, but an approach to business and human services. It is contrasted with production and sales orientations that focus on the needs of the seller (Kotler 1989). In contrast, the 'marketing concept' focuses on the needs of the buyer. It seeks profits or increased levels of participation in an activity or service, through the identification of customer needs, the development of products and services to meet these needs, and the pricing, packaging, promotion and distribution of these products in accordance with consumer habits, aspirations and expectations.

A basic distinction between social and commercial marketing is that social marketing is not usually based on needs experienced by consumers, but on needs identified by health experts (Sirgy, Morris & Samli 1985). However, a marketing approach emphasises that the development, delivery and promotion of the health message must be carried out in accordance with consumers' needs. For example, messages about immunisation must be in a language consumers understand, the promised benefits must be relevant, and the messages must be placed in media to which consumers are receptive.

2. *The concept of exchange*

The concept of exchange has long been described as the core concept of marketing: 'Marketing is the exchange which takes place between consuming groups and supplying groups' (Alderson 1957, page 15). The concept of a 'market' is therefore defined as the aggregation of individuals willing and able to engage in exchanges. The essential factor that differentiates exchanges from other forms of need satisfaction is that each party to the exchange both gains and receives value (Houston & Gassenheimer 1987). At the same time, each party perceives the offerings to involve costs. Hence it is the ratio of the perceived benefits to the costs that determines choice between alternatives (Kotler & Andreasen 1987). Kotler (1988) lists the following as necessary conditions for the *potential* for exchange:

1. There are at least two parties.
2. Each party offers something that might be of value to the other party.
3. Each party is capable of communication and delivery.
4. Each party is free to accept or reject the offer.
5. Each party believes it is appropriate or desirable to deal with the other party.

The lessons for social marketers are that we must offer something perceived to be of value to our target audiences and recognise that consumers must outlay resources such as time, money, physical comfort, lifestyle changes or psychological effort in exchange for the promised benefits (LeFebvre & Flora 1988). Furthermore, it must be remembered that all intermediaries enlisted to support the campaign (e.g. for the promotion of exercise: physicians; commercial health club operators; local community health instructors; health promotion professionals' associations; volunteer workers; sponsors), also require something of value in return for their efforts (De Musis & Miaoulis 1988). Too often, health promoters have assumed that the intermediaries' shared common goal of public health enhancement would be sufficient to ensure their support. But each intermediary should be considered a target market with his or her own needs and values that must be included in an exchange process. Hence, promotions to doctors asking them to recommend exercise to their patients must be designed with the doctors' needs in mind, that is, materials should be easy to use, easy to distribute and should improve their understanding of the area.

3. *Customer value: the concept of the marketing mix*

There are two basic concepts with respect to customer value. Firstly, customers do not just buy products or services, but rather buy benefits or bundles of benefits (Lancaster 1966). Charles Revson of Revlon said '... In the factory we make cosmetics; in the store we sell hope', and Levitt made the point that although people may buy a quarter-inch drill (the product), what they want (the benefit) is a quarter-inch hole (Kotler 1988, page 243).

Secondly, what are termed the 'four Ps' of the marketing mix, all contribute to customer value. The four Ps are: *product* (including brand name and reputation, packaging, range and types, warranties); *price* (including the monetary cost, credit terms, ease of payment (e.g. credit cards, EFTPOS)); *promotion* (including advertising, sales promotion, publicity and public relations, personal selling); and *place* or distribution (i.e. physical distribution, number and type of outlets, opening hours, atmosphere in outlets, availability of public transport, availability and ease of parking). The marketing manager's task is to blend these four elements so as to provide maximal value to particular market segments. For example, products with a high price are accompanied by extensive advertising and promotion that attempt to justify the higher price, either objectively or subjectively via appeals to sensory attributes, social status or lifestyle. Time and effort costs are reduced by making the product: easily obtained (e.g. wide distribution, vending machines in appropriate locations); able to be tried out before commitment (e.g. sample packs, in-office/in-home demonstrations, seven days free trial; easy to pay for (e.g. credit card acceptance, lay-by, hire purchase); and easy to use (e.g. user-friendly packaging, instructions on use, free training courses).

A concept that to some extent ties these two aspects (customer benefits and the four Ps) together is Kotler's (1988) concept of the *core* product, the *augmented* product and the actual *tangible* product. For example, the tangible product might be a computer. The augmented product involves the buyer's total consumption system. For computers this involves after-sales service, training, warranties, associated software, a widespread consumer–user network, and so on. The core product is better management decision making. In fact, many companies primarily compete not on tangible product features but on augmented product features (Levitt 1969).

In the health promotion of physical activity, the core product might be a longer, healthier life through reduction of the risk of cardiovascular disease, the actual product might be an aerobics class, and the augmented product might include a creche, off-peak discount rates, clean and hygienic change rooms and a complimentary towel.

4. Market segmentation: the principle of selectivity and concentration

Lunn (1986) has described segmentation as one of the most influential aspects of the marketing concept. Market segmentation involves dividing the total market into groups of individuals that are more like each other than similar individuals in other groups. The fundamental issue is to identify groups that will respond to different products or marketing strategies, and, for commercial organisations, to select and concentrate on those segments where the organisation can be most competitive.

The segmentation process involves three phases (Kotler 1989):

1. dividing the total market into segments and developing profiles of these segments
2. evaluating each segment and selecting one or more segments as target markets
3. developing a detailed marketing mix (that is, the four Ps) for each of the selected segments

SunSmart: promoting skin cancer prevention

Sponsoring body: Victorian Anti-Cancer Council.

Background: Australia has the highest rate of skin cancer in the world. The SunSmart campaign was designed to add to the very successful 'Slip!Slap!Slop!' campaign.

Objectives: Extend effects of 'Slip! Slap! Slop!' by including broader behavioural objectives involving not only hat, clothing and sunscreen use, but activity scheduling, shade provision and shade seeking.

Media: TV, radio, billboards (see illustration), brochures, public relations.

Market: Young sun-lovers.

Message: Plan for sun protection and skin cancer prevention.

Method: Advertising, publicity, public relations.

Measures: Pre- and post-test surveys showed 46% of the Victorian population were aware of the message. About half of the 48% who claimed to be taking extra protective action indicated it was because of this, or other campaigns.

VICTORIAN ANTI-CANCER COUNCIL

Source: Borland, Hill & Noy 1990.

The concept of market segmentation is fundamental to the development of communication campaigns and is dealt with in depth in Chapter 6.

5. Competition and the principle of differential advantage

In marketing, the principle of differential advantage refers to an analysis of the marketer's resources versus those of the competition, with the aim of determining where the company has an advantage over the opposition. In a wider sense it relates to monitoring and understanding competitive activity, sometimes in order to emulate or follow such activity, in other cases to pre-empt or counter competitors' activities. A study of alcohol advertising and promotion, for example, can assist in understanding appeals to young males. Advocacy groups need to monitor industries such as the tobacco industry and try to pre-empt anticipated industry moves. Similarly, health promotion organisations should identify their strengths and utilise these in developing campaigns. Commercial organisations regularly carry out SWOT analysis—audits of the organisation's *S*trengths and *W*eaknesses and analyses of *O*pportunities and *T*hreats facing the organisation as part of the strategic planning process. Health organisations should do the same when planning health promotion campaigns.

6. The environment

Commercial marketers are keenly aware that the marketing process takes place in a changing environment, and that this environment must be monitored continually, both to identify potential opportunities and to avoid potential and actual threats to the company and its products or services. Aspects of the environment that influence the marketing of goods, services and ideas are: *political/legal* (e.g. exhaust emission requirements, anti-monopoly laws, rulings on the use of words like 'natural', 'fresh'); *economic* (e.g. the introduction of low-priced alternatives during recessionary periods, changes in spending patterns); *technological* (e.g. changes in packaging and production methods, entire categories of products such as typewriters becoming obsolete); *social and cultural* (e.g. the demand for environmentally friendly packaging and products, the consumer movement, 'yearning' for traditional values); *demographic trends* (e.g. increase in single-person and single-parent households, growing Asian-born population, the ageing of the population).

7. The use of market research

Given all of the above factors, it should be apparent that effective marketing is a research-based process. Research is necessary to ascertain the different needs of different consumer segments; to test product and service prototypes against identified segments; to pretest advertising and other communication materials; to evaluate campaign outcomes; to monitor environmental influences; to assess media scheduling variables; to test packaging and price variations and the attractiveness of various potential sales incentives; to provide feedback on competitive activity and on consumer reactions to that activity; and to undertake test marketing activities. In short, research is necessary to effectively integrate all elements of the marketing mix (product, place, price and promotion) so as to apply the organisation's resources most efficiently toward meeting the needs of a defined segment or segments of a target audience.

Research in health marketing is concerned with epidemiological data and with assessment of factors such as: what health 'products' (e.g. exercise, dietary fat reduction, smoking cessation) does the community perceive as priorities for action; what *tangible* products can be developed to facilitate the adoption of health-promoting behaviour or to reduce risk (e.g. no-tar cigarettes, low fat foods, quit smoking kits, exercise videos); what programs or services can be offered (e.g. weight control, aerobics classes, educational videos on the benefits of exercise, training videos on how to institute worksite programs); how products and programs should be packaged, priced, positioned, promoted and distributed; how the message strategy should be developed; what social and structural facilitators and inhibitors need to be taken into account; who are the relevant influencers and intermediaries; what media (television, radio, press) and what media vehicles (specific programs), if any, can be used to cost-effectively reach the target audience(s); and what activities are being undertaken by 'anti-health' marketers.

The major use of research in social marketing campaigns has been primarily in the development and pretesting of communication materials (advertising, posters, brochures, community service announcements), measures of exposure to campaign materials, and pre-post surveys or periodic surveys to assess changes in attitudes, beliefs and behaviours over the duration of the campaign (see Chapter 12).

8. An integrated planning process

Although we have listed a number of key marketing concepts separately, it should be clear that these are interrelated and interdependent. This represents another key aspect of the marketing process—it is an *integrated* process in which the elements of the marketing mix, the organisation's resources, the use of market research, and the selection and concentration on specific market segments are all combined to maximise the value of the organisation's offerings to the consumer. This, in turn, produces profit for a company, or the changes in knowledge, attitude or behaviour sought by a health organisation.

This integration strongly implies the need for a systematic strategic planning process: the setting of clearly defined overall goals; the setting of measurable objectives to meet the overall goals; the delineation of strategies and tactics to achieve these objectives; and management and feedback systems to ensure that the plan is implemented as desired and problems are averted or dealt with as they arise (see Chapter 13).

Differences between commercial and social marketing: can we sell health like we sell soap?

PRINCIPLES AND PRACTICES of marketing are clearly applicable to the promotion of healthy lifestyles, but it is a mistake to assume that social marketing is similar to commercial marketing in all respects. Even within marketing, different approaches are more or less appropriate for different products. In short, while some of the principles of marketing are applicable, selling health or any other socially desirable 'product' can not be fully equated with 'selling soap' (Wiebe 1952).

Bloom and Novelli (1981) and Rothschild (1979) list a number of important differences between the marketing of commercial products and social marketing. The major differences are:

1. Commercial products tend to offer instant gratification, whereas the benefits of many health behaviours are often delayed.
2. Social marketing attempts to replace undesirable behaviours with behaviours that are often more costly in time or effort and, at least in the short term, less pleasurable or even unpleasant.

3. Commercial marketing mostly aims at groups already positive towards the product and its benefits, whereas social marketing is frequently directed towards hard-to-reach, at-risk groups who are often those most antagonistic to change.

4. Health risk behaviours are often extremely complex, both at a personal and social level, and are far more so than the behaviours involved in purchasing most commercial products.

5. Intermediaries in commercial marketing are far fewer in type and generally far easier to deal with (although perhaps more costly) than in social marketing.

6. Defining and communicating the 'product' is far more difficult in social marketing, especially where experts may have different views on the subject.

7. The exchange process is far easier to define in commercial marketing than in social marketing.

8. Many targeted health behaviours are inconsistent with social pressures.

9. Ethical questions and issues of equity are far more complex and important (e.g. 'victim blaming') in social marketing.

10. Social marketing should also be directed not only towards changes in individual behaviour, but also towards changes in systems and social structures that operate to the detriment of the health of populations.

Social marketing attempts to change complex behaviours

Concepts from marketing that are relevant to media-based health promotion campaigns have been categorised here into the five Ms of social marketing as it applies to health: *medium, market, message, method* and *measures*. In Part 2 of this book we elaborate on each of these, giving detailed perspectives for practical implementation.

PART 2

Practices

4

INTRODUCTION TO PART 2

A framework for using the media in health promotion

THERE ARE MANY different ways of examining the use of the media in promoting health. In this book we have chosen a social marketing context because it provides the best understanding of how to use the media to influence behaviour and, more significantly, because it is a *process* for organising interventions. As Novelli (1984) points out, marketing ' . . . provides a framework for moving in an orderly, disciplined fashion from a to z'. We have distilled the core elements of the media-related components of a social marketing program into what we call the five Ms: *medium, market, message, method* and *measures*. These provide the structure for the core of the practical section of this book.

Medium refers to 'the means by which something is communicated' (the *Oxford Dictionary*). It thus defines a mechanism of communication which can range from printed material to sophisticated electronic devices. A classification of media types and their specific characteristics for health promotion follows in Chapter 5.

The *market* consists of the target audiences for whom a communication is intended. Markets can be segmented on a number of different bases. The bases, processes and concepts of market segmentation for health promotion are considered in Chapter 6.

The *message* content of any communication forms the core of that communication. Developing a message to satisfy an objective is not simply a matter of 'having something to say', but knowing 'how best to say it' (see Chapter 7). Many messages are inextricably linked with production techniques and some of the specialist skills this involves are considered in Chapter 8.

Method refers to the mode of delivery of a message. There are a number of different ways of using the media in health promotion. This book concentrates on the three major methods used in health and social change promotion:

1. Advertising (Chapter 9)
2. Publicity (Chapter 10)

3. 'Edutainment' (Chapter 11)

As these form the core of the practical section of the book, each is defined and described below, and a framework for their operation explained.

The *measures* considered in Chapter 13 cover the areas of formative research, efficacy testing, process evaluation and outcome evaluation.

Defining methods

Advertising

Advertising generally refers to the *paid* placement of messages in various media vehicles by an identified source. We include as advertising situations where media organisations donate time or space for the placement of social change messages that are clearly in the form of advertisements. These are known as 'community' (or in the United States 'public') service announcements (CSAs or PSAs). By law, advertisements must be identified as such, and in most cases are clearly distinguishable from the programming (electronic media) or editorial (print media) content of the media vehicle. There are a large number of advertising media available, ranging from the rear of toilet doors, to shopping centre noticeboards, to national television networks. The types of media available are listed in Chapter 5.

Based on a small number of large-scale mass-intervention studies that made extensive use of the media in health in the 1970s and early 1980s, an advertising approach to using the media, involving paid and unpaid media spots, was widely experimented with. This resulted in several campaigns in countries such as Australia, the United Kingdom and Canada where paid advertising constituted the major component of projects in areas such as smoking, alcohol, nutrition and AIDS prevention.

Publicity

The cost of advertising campaigns can be prohibitive and this has led to health promotion practitioners paying more attention to unpaid media methods to get their message across. Many campaigns now involve press conferences with celebrities and staged events that attract considerable coverage by the media. These events can be supported by activities such as providing the media with feature articles (for newspapers and magazines) and making experts available for interview on radio and television. This use of the media is one of the tools of *public relations* and is known as *publicity*.

Public relations refers to the activities that an organisation undertakes to create and maintain positive relations with all of its 'public' including customers, staff, suppliers, journalists and politicians (Belch & Belch 1990).

Publicity refers to the *unpaid* placement of messages in the media, usually in news or current affairs programs, but also in feature articles or documentaries. Unlike advertising, the source of the message is seen to be a presumably unbiased journalist rather than the organisation whose product or message is the subject of the news item or feature.

Publicity involves attracting the media to run a particular story or cover a particular event in a way that creates, maintains or increases the target audience's awareness of, or favourable attitudes towards, the organisation's products or message, or towards the organisation itself. Events can be staged to deliberately attract attention, and media organisations can be provided with support materials such as press releases, videotapes, feature articles and photographs.

'Edutainment'

A third, and increasing use of the media for health promotion is the deliberate inclusion of socially desirable messages in entertainment vehicles such as television soap operas, in order to achieve some social change objective (Montgomery 1990; Singhal & Rogers 1989). For example, the Harvard alcohol project in the United States approached television writers to introduce into top-rated TV programs, actions and themes that would reinforce and encourage a social norm that drivers don't drink. The project has obtained the co-operation of 15 Hollywood studios and the three major United States television networks (DeJong & Winsten 1990). This strategy, called 'edutainment' by some writers, has been used mainly in Third World countries, but recent observations suggest a likely substantial increase in the use of the strategy in developed countries, including Australia (Davern 1991).

Choosing media methods

THE DECISION OF whether to use advertising, publicity or edutainment, or some combination of these, in any health promotion campaign is determined by such things as the objectives of the campaign, the budget, the relative effectiveness of the different modes in reaching and impacting on the target audiences, the complexity of the message, time constraints, relations with the media, and the nature and types of media and media vehicles available.

From the campaign manager's perspective, the primary advantages of paid advertising relate to control factors—that is, control over message content, message exposure (timing and 'location', and hence target audience) and frequency of exposure. Control over message content not only allows precise specification of the information content of the message, but (and especially with regard to publicity) also allows the creation of imagery and the use of various message execution techniques and appeals that enhance the persuasive power of the message.

Advertising's major disadvantage is cost, both production costs (though creative advertising people can, and do develop messages that do not require expensive production) and media scheduling costs (by far the larger component). However, because the number of people exposed to advertising is usually quite large, the cost per individual contact and impact is often quite low, especially when compared with face-to-face methods.

Publicity and edutainment share the ability of advertising to reach large numbers of people in a relatively short period of time, but have the disadvantage of less control over message content, message exposure and frequency (unless the theme continues for several episodes in a soap opera, or the issue is sufficiently newsworthy to attract continuing coverage for several days). A press release, for example, might be rewritten in a way that omits or distorts crucial information, be relegated to the later pages of a newspaper, only appear in a very late news spot, or even be totally ignored.

On the other hand, publicity is generally perceived as more credible than paid advertising (because the source is presumably unbiased, or less biased), and is less costly. However, costs are incurred in developing materials or staging events and often there are fees for engaging professional public relations agencies.

The primary advantage of edutainment (which also, but to a lesser extent applies to publicity), is the ability to attract the attention of people who might otherwise deliberately avoid messages that appear in some other form. Where a health authority or sponsoring body is not directly involved in producing the show, edutainment can be quite inexpensive. However, where a health organisation is a joint or sole producer, costs can be very high. On the other hand, if a show is a commercial success, the health organisation can even earn a profit (Coleman & Meyer 1990).

Roles of the media in health promotion campaigns

THE MASS MEDIA components of health promotion campaigns can be designed to achieve a number of objectives. However there appear to be *three major roles* , two of which apply primarily to the targeting of individual behaviour change and one to the achievement of socio-political objectives.

A fourth role is a 'directing' or 'public announcement' role—that is, the media carry messages directing people to some service or event. In this case the information is not about the health issue in question but directs people to further information about the issue (e.g. promoting a telephone information service), to activities associated with the issue (e.g. a Quit sponsored 'fun run'), or to opportunities for community involvement in policy making (e.g. announcing a public meeting to deal with local health issues).

Roles for targeting individual behaviour change

The two primary communication objectives for the media components of the vast majority of campaigns that *target individual behaviour change*, whether via paid advertising, publicity or edutainment, are (Donovan 1991):

To inform (or educate)
To persuade (or motivate)

By inform, or educate we mean that the communication objectives are to create or maintain awareness, knowledge and understanding of the health issue in question. By persuade or motivate, we mean that the communication objectives, achieved via emotional arousal, are to induce attitude change, behavioural intentions or explicit actions on the part of the recipient of the message (Rossiter & Percy 1987).

Most campaigns will include both of these objectives, although some may emphasise one or the other. Furthermore, different campaign components will best perform one or other of these roles. Advertising is mainly associated with persuasion, whereas most public health pamphlets, especially in years gone by, have focused on education.

The distinction between these two roles is blurred in that information is generally not provided for its own sake, but is usually meant to lead to desired behaviour changes. However, while information alone can arouse emotions and motivate *some* people to cease an unhealthy practice, it is clear from both the smoking (see Flay 1987) and the AIDS literature (see Edgar, Freimuth & Hammond 1988), that information in itself is insufficient to bring about desired behaviour changes in *most* individuals.

Increasing evidence that knowledge alone was insufficient to achieve attitude and behaviour changes amongst substantial proportions of the population led public health officials to focus more attention on how to improve the motivational power of their health messages. This led to the commissioning of marketing communications experts to apply the persuasion techniques of marketing to health behaviours. Many of these initial efforts were ineffective because the marketers lacked an understanding of the more complex health behaviours relative to most consumer purchasing behaviours. At the same time, health professionals lacked an adequate understanding of the discipline of marketing and the principles of communication that were required to adequately brief, evaluate and control the marketing and advertising professionals. Many health professionals at the time simply assumed that mass media *advertising* was the 'magic key' to success. Advertising agencies, perhaps understandably, did little to convince them otherwise.

While the techniques and principles of marketing are applicable to any consumer decision, their effective application to health promotion requires an understanding of both areas. In practical terms this requires close co-operation between marketing experts, public health professionals and, for mass media campaign components, behavioural scientists with expertise in communication theory, and attitude and behaviour change.

Targeting socio-political change: media advocacy

Most uses of the mass media in health promotion have been directed towards individual risk behaviour change. However, along with other efforts more associated with the practice of lobbying, the mass media also have been used to achieve socio-political environmental changes that affect health. For example, the quit smoking lobby—those most associated with media advocacy to date—have used the media to redefine smoking as a public health issue of concern to all, and to attack the morals and motives of tobacco companies' marketing techniques. The subsequent arousal of public opinion has been used to support direct lobbying for legislative changes with respect to restricting the advertising of cigarettes and the sponsorship of sporting and cultural events by tobacco companies. This use of the media—which is being increasingly promoted as a health promotion tool, particularly for arousing community action—represents its third major role:

To advocate

Media advocacy has been defined (Wallack 1990, page 158) as:

> . . . a range of strategies to stimulate broad-based media coverage in order to reframe public debate to increase public support for more effective policy level approaches to public health problems.

It can be described as the use of media, usually via unpaid publicity, to place a particular point of view before the public with respect to some controversial issue, with the aim of involving the public in the resolution of that issue. While educational and motivational objectives tend to focus on individual risk behaviours, advocacy objectives tend to focus on broader socio-political factors that impinge on individuals' and communities' opportunities and capacities to achieve an improved health status. Furthermore, a major aim of media advocacy is to empower the public to take part in policy making. Media advocacy attempts to arouse the public and to encourage social action groups to take an active role in the political process, both at the local community level and at a state or national level. Such an aim is most often associated with grassroots activist groups with little funds. However, media advocacy is used by a great variety of organisations.

The recognition of environmental influences on health is, of course, not new. As far back as the Middle Ages the association between socio-environmental conditions and individuals' physical and mental health have been acknowledged (Holman 1992). What is new is the attempt to initiate direct public participation in the development and implementation of public health policy (see boxed text).

The media advocacy approach to health promotion is often contrasted with, or presented as an alternative to the social marketing approach (e.g. Wallack 1990). The former primarily makes use of unpaid publicity, whereas the latter is mostly associated with paid advertising. However, this distinction, as with many other perceived distinctions between the two approaches, is not exclusive to either approach. Social marketing *can* and *does* make use of unpaid publicity, and media advocacy campaigns *can* and *do* make use of paid advertising and/or CSAs.

While many large commercial organisations, including tobacco companies, and some well-funded health authorities can afford to use paid advertising in their advocacy campaigns, most health professionals have to rely on unpaid publicity (see Fox 1986). This is particularly so in the United States where the federal and many state govern-

Advocacy, advertising

**Cut this out
and put it
in bed next to
your child.**

The headline and rat shown above formed the basis of a 1967 advertising campaign devised by two US ad agency people who were incensed by the US Congress's rejection of a 'rat extermination' bill. The bill would have provided substantial funding for rat control in inner-city slums. The two men set up their own ad hoc organisation to have the bill introduced in Congress, and to shift the vote in favour of the bill.

A continuing campaign was planned for the ad, but after two appearances in low-readership publications (one a local weekly newspaper), the ad attracted the attention of the national media. It was then shown on television, read on radio and appeared as news in magazines and newspapers across the nation. The bill was reintroduced and passed.

The ad also listed all members of Congress and how they originally voted. Readers were urged to write in support of those who had voted 'yes' (a positive action often overlooked in the rush to address those opposed to our desires), and to ask those who had voted against the bill to change their mind.

ments are opposed in principle to the use of paid advertising. The United States National AIDS Information and Education campaign, which produces television, print and radio PSAs for national distribution, must rely on donated time and space for exposure (Woods, Davis & Westover 1991; Donovan, Jason, Gibbs & Kroger 1991).

Individual and socio-political change objectives should be combined for any comprehensive health campaign. However, in some cases individual-targeted campaigns must have the first impact, at least on beliefs and attitudes towards the recommended behaviour, before socio-political advocacy objectives can be achieved. For example, it is unlikely that efforts to present smoking as a public health issue would have been as successful without prior Quit campaigns that emphasised the connection between smoking and ill-health. Similarly, efforts to control smoking indoors were undoubtedly facilitated by increasing awareness of the effects of passive smoking. Legal recognition of these effects will accelerate restrictions on smoking indoors.

A structure for media use in health promotion

THREE MAJOR METHODS of media use (advertising, publicity and edutainment) and three major roles or objectives of mass media campaign messages (educate, motivate and advocate) have been described. As shown in Table 4.1, each of these methods can be utilised to promote any of these overall objectives.

Table 4.1
A structure for media use in health promotion

	Method		
	Advertising	Publicity	Edutainment
Individual Objectives			
Inform or educate		(Behaviour change)	
Persuade or motivate		(Behaviour change)	
Social Objectives			
Advocate		(Social/structural change)	

We will now proceed to describe the ways in which these methods can be used and objectives achieved.

The Medium

A MEDIUM IS the means by which a message is communicated. Mass media are the means for communicating to large numbers (masses) of people. Australia in the early 1990s is served by about 65 television stations, 446 radio stations and 34 major newspapers, as well as numerous suburban, regional and ethnic papers and trade, general and specialty magazines and newsletters. (Information about media is regularly updated in *Media Ownership in Australia* published by Information Australia, Margaret Gee Media Group).

The major types of media and their sub-types are summarised in the table below. All of these can play a role in health promotion in different situations.

Types of media

Type of transmission	Type of medium	Sub-type
A. Electronic	Television	National, regional, closed circuit, cable, video
	Radio	National (ABC), national (network), metropolitan, regional, AM/FM, ethnic, public access, local
	Cinema	National distribution, limited distribution, mainstream, 'cult'
	Telecommunications	Telephone, fax, electronic mail
B. Print	Newspapers	National, major metropolitan, rural, local, community, special interest, ethnic, daily, weekly, Sunday only
	Magazines	National broad audience, specific interest, trade and professional, weekly, monthly
	Pamphlets, brochures	Government, commercial
	Posters, fridge stickers	Government, commercial
C. Outdoor	Billboards	Roadside, sporting events, cultural events
	Signs, posters	Bus sides, taxi backs, T-shirts, bumper stickers
D. Direct mail		Own client lists, purchased lists

A number of more broadly based classifications of the media have been made over the years, some of which identify the ways in which various media function—for example:

- *mass* versus *limited* reach (e.g. television, national magazines versus pamphlets, T-shirts, posters, stickers)

- *passive* versus *active* (e.g. television, radio versus newspapers)
- *broadcasting* versus *narrowcasting* (e.g. television, radio versus cable, video, newsletters)
- *'hot'* versus *'cool'* (e.g. television versus magazines)
- *ex-home* versus *in-home* (e.g. cinema, outdoor versus radio, television)
- *two-way* versus *one-way* (e.g. talkback radio, interactive video versus cinema, television)

Primary and secondary media

MOST PAID ADVERTISING campaigns make use of a primary medium, into which most of the promotional effort is put, and one or more secondary media (Rossiter & Percy 1987). Publicity campaigns should also comprise primary and secondary media.

The primary medium is selected because it is the single most cost-effective medium for reaching and impacting the target audience(s) for a campaign. For large-scale national campaigns, the primary medium would almost always be television if cost was not a limiting factor. Exceptions to this are campaigns that impart detailed information. For this purpose, and with cost taken into consideration, the pamphlet or brochure has become one of the most common primary media in health promotion—despite a lack of convincing evidence that this is the most cost-effective approach (Donovan 1987).

Secondary media are used as back-up for the primary medium, particularly in the following circumstances: (a) where a section of the target audience is not reached by the primary medium (e.g. infrequent television viewers, non-readers of pamphlets); (b) where communication objectives can be achieved at lower cost with a medium other than the primary medium (e.g. using a television ad soundtrack on the much cheaper medium of radio); (c) where support is needed for the primary medium closer to the point of decision (e.g. re-assuring brochures about immunisation for children can reduce a mother's anxiety at, or just before visiting an immunisation centre).

The description of the media that follows in Chapter 5 includes a discussion of the advantages and disadvantages of the major categories of media in relation to health promotion.

5

Describing the media

I N THIS CHAPTER, each of the major media in the table on page 51 will be discussed in general terms only. Specific channels, for example rural television, local newspapers in rural regions, ethnic newspapers, can have individual and idiosyncratic characteristics over and above those considered here. An overall summary of the characteristics of each media type is presented in Table 5.1 at the end of the chapter.

A. Electronic media

ELECTRONIC MEDIA ARE generally considered to be 'hot' (McLuhan 1964) or emotive in contrast to the 'cooler', cognitive medium of print. While electronic media can provide information, the amount of information is limited by the transient nature of the medium per se (i.e. there is little opportunity to rehearse, reread or relisten to the information in a news item or documentary—unless it is videotaped), and because of the costs involved in presenting large amounts of information in paid time. Electronic media are therefore used to most effect to create 'heat' (motivation or interest) about an issue rather than to shed 'light' on that issue. In this sense, electronic media serve to sensitise or direct the audience to further sources of information or intervention. Electronic campaigns are supported by accompanying print and related materials.

1. Television

Television is perhaps the 'hottest' of the 'hot' media. It is highly visible, intrusive and ubiquitous—about 90% of Australian households have at least one television set and this includes lower-income groups and now even remote-area Aboriginal communities (Spark et al. 1988). Although the main role of television in health promotion is often seen as one of 'agenda setting'—that is, placing the issue on the community's agenda (Maccoby et al. 1980), there is little doubt that in some circumstances direct behaviour change can be initiated (Puska et al. 1987).

Because of its intrusiveness and immediacy, television lends itself to creating widespread awareness of issues, as well as contributing to the formation of opinions and attitudes. Health issues such as smoking, where knowledge about ill-effects is widespread and the adoption of behaviour is influenced by social norms, are well suited to television (Flay 1987). The intrusive nature of television is an advantage in situations where the target audience may selectively disregard messages that may make them feel uncomfortable about their unhealthy behaviours.

Another advantage of television is that, alone amongst all the media, it combines sight, sound and movement. Television is therefore ideally suited to the modelling of desirable behaviours, whether in short message structures such as advertising, or in longer presentations such as soap opera episodes. While print is the major medium for communicating comprehensive information, television news and documentary programs can be used to provide substantial amounts of information. University of the air programs are an example of this. On the other hand, television advertisements, because they are limited to 30 or 60 seconds, rarely provide comprehensive information, but can highlight major issues in a simplified way (e.g. 'cholesterol is associated with heart disease'), and to direct or sensitise the audience to more comprehensive information from other sources (e.g. magazine articles or consultation with a GP). Notwithstanding the above limitations, television has the ability, via graphics and concrete demonstrations, to simplify complex processes.

Print media have the ability to communicate beliefs and images through the use of non-verbal, visual symbols, while radio has the ability to do this with music and sound effects (sfx). Television, because it combines both of these attributes, is clearly superior in this regard. The ability to communicate symbolically is one reason why voluntary codes of advertising often have little effect: promises in strict verbal form can be broken because of the interpretation—conscious or sub-conscious—which is placed on a visual image by the viewer.

Audience surveys suggest that there are two types of media users: those who derive most of their information and entertainment from television, and those who derive most of their information and entertainment from print media, with a lower socio-economic bias towards the former (Crask & Reynolds 1980). Hence, television has an added advantage where lower socio-economic target groups are included.

The major disadvantages of television are its 'perishability' (advertising campaigns are short-lived) and the cost of advertising. However, with increased nationalisation and regionalisation of television services throughout Australia, the cost per effective transmission is reduced when the large audience reach which can be achieved is considered. Furthermore, viewers with VCRs can be encouraged to record and play special health programs. Television is a passive medium in that, apart from distractions and deliberate interruptions, once a program is chosen the viewer has no control over delivery of the message. On the other hand, print is an active medium because the reader determines what will be read in depth or what will be merely glanced at.

In summary, the use of television for health promotion is appropriate in situations where budgetary constraints are not limited and/or for short, intensive campaigns. It appears *best* suited for:

- modelling of health behaviours
- reaching large audiences rapidly
- creating awareness of an issue amongst audiences who might ignore the message in other media
- getting emotive or personal messages across
- providing complex information in simple graphical form
- reaching lower socio-economic groups

The main forms of health promotion through television are advertising spots and community service announcements (CSAs), news items, current affairs, documentaries, information briefs in entertainment programs, and the inclusion of health messages in soap operas (edutainment).

2. Radio

The advent of television in the 1950s led to predictions that radio was finished as a medium. While it is now obvious that this is not true, it is clear that radio had to shift its orientation to co-exist with television. Radio decreased its role as a source of 'heavy' entertainment (e.g. drama, serialisation) and increased its role as a source of news, information and 'light' entertainment (e.g. music). Two recent developments have further distinguished modern from traditional radio. Firstly, the development of talk-back radio has made the medium even more intimate and personal. Individuals are able to air their opinions, get instant 'expert' advice on a range of topics from health to handy homemaker hints, and to get feedback on their views from other members of the community, without ever leaving home. Secondly, the introduction of Frequency Modulation (FM) radio in the 1980s, with its ability to produce better-quality musical sound, led to some AM stations specialising more in news, information and specialty programming. This style of programming is particularly suited to informative-style health promotion.

Radio stations differ far more from each other in the style and content of their programs than do the television stations. Australian metropolitan radio stations, for example, are characterised by quite distinct target audiences. Rival stations, in order to compete for the advertising dollar, have developed programming to meet the needs of specific target audiences. Hence radio is ideally suited for targeting specific groups, including ethnic and Aboriginal groups.

Radio advertising, because of its relative affordability (it is much cheaper than television) and ability to reach specific target audiences, is an ideal medium for frequent-reminder advertising concerning specific behaviours. For example, evening drive-time radio can be used to target drivers for drink-driving messages; teenage audiences can be targeted just prior to weekends for safe sex and anti-alcohol-bingeing messages. Teenagers are considerably less-regular viewers of television and readers of newspapers than adults, but they are far greater listeners to radio. Hence radio is an ideal medium for messages to teenagers in the vernacular of pop music.

The impact of radio might be expected to be less than that of television. However, the impact is likely to be more sustainable on radio (because of lower costs), and topics merely broached on television can be expanded on radio to achieve a deeper understanding of issues. For this reason, radio is a good secondary medium where television is used as the primary medium. It does have a role as a primary medium though, particularly in country areas where one radio station is predominant. Radio also has wider exposure through its portability, inclusion in cars, and use throughout the night by a significant proportion of the population. Radio is also more desirable in terms of advertising and program content, especially when compared with television, because time can be bought and ads can be developed (or changed) very close to the time of airing. Similarly, talkback topics can be varied with little notice and in response to the latest news topics.

Advertisements on radio (including CSAs) can be lost in the clutter of advertising, and may even go unnoticed on stations only listened to for background music. Radio is best used for publicity in news events, talkback programs, and ads on programs where the audience is listening attentively to the program content.

Radio is limited by its perishability and by its inability to show images (e.g. social approval, sensory gratification of foods), although this can be countered to some extent by descriptive and creative copywriting or by image transfer from television promotions to radio promotions where radio is used as the secondary medium. It also has distinct advantages for making longer-term exposure possible, for cost effectiveness and for its flexibility.

In summary, radio is an effective medium for:

- extended exposure
- intellectual stimulation
- local issues
- back-up support for television
- 'expert' interaction
- immediate feedback
- medium-budget campaigns
- contact with the socially and physically isolated

The main uses of radio for health promotion are paid spots, daytime and late night talkback and commentary, and feature programs (e.g. leisure activities, health).

3. Video

As with many innovations, the increase in the ownership of video recorders (to the extent that 60% of Australian homes possessed video recorders in 1990) suggested big opportunities for health promotion. Many major health issues could be covered in-depth by video in a way which was expected to be immediately popular amongst a wide target audience.

Initial reactions to the early proliferation of health videos indicates that this may have been an overly optimistic assumption. Although videos have the potential to contain much valuable information, they have the disadvantage of being time consuming and hence require a high level of motivation which is usually not present in the average viewer for general health issues. Although it is still early days, the best use of video for health promotion in the home is likely to be amongst specialist target groups (e.g. diabetics, home exercise devotees, asthmatics). The development of inter-active video (e.g. where the viewer can make a response which influences the outcome of the video) presents an interesting future opportunity for training in health and health promotion.

Possible locations for video outside the home include doctors' waiting rooms, corrective institutions and hospitals (where a captive audience may be motivated), and schools and public lectures (as an audio-visual aid). Lack of attention span in large groups makes the use of videos, other than those which are short and informative, a poor medium for group interventions. The Doctors' Television Network (DTV), currently operating in Australia (see Chapter 11) is an example of the value of video in the 'captive audience' situation (i.e. doctors' waiting rooms).

In summary, although the prospects for home video in health promotion may have been oversold, video does have potential for:
- specialist health topics (e.g. diabetes, back care, exercise)
- captive audiences (e.g. doctors' waiting rooms, hospitals, schools)

4. Computers

To date, computers have been used primarily for production and computation rather than communication. Hence there has been little consideration of computers as a medium for transmitting health messages. The development of new technologies such as on-line databases, information systems, voice mail and electronic mail which can be accessed from home computers by telephone has made this a more feasible health promotion medium for the future. Already, systems provide recorded health information for on-line subscribers. A further use of computers is the possible widespread availability of self-care health programs (e.g. fitness testing , dietary analysis, risk factor analysis).

B. Print media

PRINT MEDIA INCLUDE *mass reach* (newspapers, magazines) and *limited reach* vehicles (e.g. pamphlets, brochures). In general, print is most effective in situations where 'light' rather than 'heat' (i.e. knowledge versus emotion) is required, although it is now acknowledged that at least in advertising, emotive issues can also be tackled effectively in print. Print, unlike electronic media, is non-intrusive and passive, and hence there is a greater need for attention-getting headlines, pictures or graphics to capture an audience. Paid print advertising varies in cost according to readership, but is generally less expensive than electronic media.

Less-expensive print media include limited reach vehicles such as local newspapers, brochures, pamphlets, fact sheets, booklets and newsletters. The trade-off here is in cost versus coverage, although in some cases coverage can be expanded by the use of direct mail (see below) or inclusion in wider-circulation media (e.g. brochures as inserts, or feature articles in magazines or newspapers). The use of brochures in local newspapers has been found to be an effective, but perhaps overlooked, means of distribution of such materials (Collins 1989).

1. Newspapers and magazines

While newsprint might be informative and helpful in increasing the spread of a campaign, this is generally short-lived and use of this medium thus needs to be considered on a cost-impact basis. Suburban and weekend newspapers extend the life of a communication, although decreased penetration of the former and increased cost of the latter are the trade-offs. In general, newspaper articles and features are best for health topics where knowledge gain is important and lengthy copy is necessary (e.g. nutrition, lifestyle, new health findings). Newspaper ads which are informative are likely to be most effective. Emotion-arousing print ads are likely to be more effective if print is secondary to electronic media promotions of a similar kind.

Newspaper news is an effective way of creating awareness (sometimes by 'beating up' or re-exposing old stories) and informing about events. Editorial support in a newspaper is one of the most effective uses of the medium because it provides evidence of 'social proof' (Cialdini 1984). If a newspaper expresses an opinion, this suggests a large proportion of the readership would be of like mind. A disadvantage of editorials is that editorial discretion may lie with the editor or publisher alone. Newspapers now have different sections (e.g. sport, lifestyle, business) which target different sections of the community and thereby offer a more effective means of reaching a target audience.

General magazines (e.g. *Women's Weekly, Time*) provide a greater depth of coverage of news, events and issues. Like Sunday newspapers, they are read at a more leisurely pace than daily newspapers which are often just skimmed for the major topical news events. This applies particularly to full-time employed persons. Special magazines (e.g. *Wheels, PC Weekly*) provide a means of communicating with specialist target audiences (e.g. sportspersons, teenagers, motorists). They are 'psychographically' selective, in contrast to newspapers which are usually more geographically selective. A further advantage of magazines is their reach and permanence, with readership extending beyond the initial target and date for extended periods through 'incidental' readership (e.g. in doctors' waiting rooms, public transport).

A disadvantage is that magazines, because of the high cost of production, are not localised, and they are therefore generally viable only for national campaigns. This also means they are likely to be expensive for paid promotions. Magazine editors, however, are always on the lookout for ideas and are often prepared to pay for articles or at least co-operate in publishing them if they are of a sufficiently high quality. Brochure ideas can sometimes also be published in magazine form.

2. Brochures, pamphlets, fact sheets, booklets

Brochures, pamphlets, fact sheets or booklets (handouts) have been the traditional means of informing about a specific topic or idea. In the commercial world, handouts represent an opportunity to bridge the gap between interest being shown in a product and the purchase of that product. In health, the handout represents a means of cost-effectively summarising an issue and/or affecting the outcome of an action.

Handouts are best used when cognition rather than emotion is the desired outcome, and more so where an action consequence is the desired outcome (e.g. completing a coupon for more information, attending a course). Handouts generally serve an educational function and often accompany more active education, such as in a doctor's or dentist's surgery or a community health centre. This is not to say that handouts should be bland or that they should not incorporate a creative or emotional component in their appeal.

In general, when a handout is being produced, the more resistant a behaviour is to change, the greater the creative requirement; the more the need for information, the less the need for creative copy (although an attractive, stimulating presentation will always be more effective than a dull, bland presentation). Handouts on alcohol or drug use, for example, require a greater emotional 'hook' than handouts on chlamydia or immunisation.

Distribution of handouts is a key factor in their potential success. While specific-issue handouts for a motivated audience (e.g. breast feeding by new mothers) can effectively be left in locations where that audience would be expected to gather, other

> ### *The use and abuse of pamphlets*
>
> The pamphlet has been the bread and butter of the health educator. But a large proportion of pamphlets, produced without detailed background research, are at best ineffective and, at worst, totally useless. A pamphlet can be an inexpensive, effective way to impart knowledge to a specific target audience looking for that information. A pamphlet can be likened to a bus timetable: for anyone wishing to catch a bus it's a valuable document, but for a car driver or train traveller it has little value until such time as there's a train strike or a car breakdown.

topics (e.g. dietary fibre consumption in the aged) may require more creative distribution—through doctors' surgeries, chemists, supermarket checkout counters, magazine inserts, or via direct mail.

Handouts are generally free, but a small fee for more desirable handouts can increase the motivation to use these (e.g. nutritional recipe books as used in the West Australian Health Department's 'Eat Less Fat' campaign: see Chapter 7). Distribution can be increased through co-operation with a suitable commercial product.

The choice between pamphlet, brochure, fact sheet or booklet depends on topic, target audience and budget. In general, handouts are best distributed through professional service outlets (e.g. chemists, doctors) and are most suited to:

- backing up other media, at reasonable cost
- providing information about specific topics
- backing up other active education
- stimulating desired action outcomes
- summarising detailed information

> ### *Flash it on a poster*
>
> Posters generally allow limited opportunity for detailed scrutiny. They are either seen (quickly) in passing, while doing something else (e.g. talking, eating, drinking), or from a distance that doesn't allow close attention to detail. A poster should aim to reinforce a slogan or logo, present an image that creates an emotional reaction to the subject, or serve as a back-up to other aspects of a campaign. Where information is provided, it should be brief, clearly written, legible (e.g. in large type) and preferably illustrated
>
>

3. Other print media

This includes items such as newsletters, indoor posters, stickers, T-shirts and general merchandise.

In recent years the interest in newsletters has increased, and these represent a means of maintaining continuity with a target audience. Newsletters can provide a sense of importance to the receiver who feels she/he is the receiver of privileged information. Hence the newsletter needs to be carefully targeted (usually through direct mail).

Special topic newsletters (e.g. on finance, health) are usually sold at a minimum rate of about three times their cost in order to be profitable. The expense adds to the feeling of exclusiveness, but obviously limits this medium as a means of communication with low-income individuals. Free newsletters are not regarded with the same esteem and are more likely to be seen as throwaways than valued, collectable information. Desktop publishing systems now make newsletters and other media, such as handouts, easy and inexpensive to produce. However, a major problem with newsletters is maintaining the momentum of the publisher's initial enthusiasm. Newsletters are an 'active' medium and therefore do not target groups uninterested in the message.

Sticking your message down

Bumper stickers, fridge magnets and other forms of message attachment confirm the commitment of an individual or group to the message. It also reinforces the individual's view of him or herself through explicit display.

T-shirts and stickers (e.g. bumper stickers, fridge magnets), like newsletters, provide a user with a distinct feeling of identity in an increasingly anonymous world. T-shirt and sticker messages help to confirm attitudes and build the commitment of the user to a campaign target theme. They are therefore useful secondary, and even tertiary, media in any campaign. These media also extend the permanence of a campaign by the continual reminder of a topic theme and the social proof that such a theme is having effect at the personal level.

T-shirts: a mobile message of commitment

T-shirt messages grew out of the 1970s when obvious commitment to a cause was fashionable. Advertisers quickly realised the advantages of this form of communication. Often it was a way of getting people to actually pay for advertising their product. As pointed out by Cialdini (1984), commitment is one of the most effective tools of influence.

The T-shirt has now become an established way to subtly diffuse a message through society, often via converts to the cause.

Stickers are the 'fun' side of a promotion and because of their collectable value they are popular, particularly with children. To be effective, however, stickers need to be either visually stimulating or verbally catchy, and they therefore require professional creative input.

Posters throughout history have had an agenda-setting function (e.g. 'Uncle Sam Needs You'). Although the poster has been relegated to a secondary status by more sophisticated media in advanced countries, it still represents an effective visual reinforcement for an idea or campaign. Like stickers and T-shirts, the art of poster creation is a complex one and should be left to creative experts, although the basic communication goals need to be understood. A major limitation to the use of posters is the expense of producing and printing quality material. This can sometimes be covered if there is sponsorship by a related product (e.g. a breakfast cereal sponsoring dietary fibre). The main function of many indoor posters in western societies is emotive rather than informative. Hence the content should be primarily visual, not verbal.

In summary, the use of T-shirts, stickers and posters is best for:

- support of a campaign theme
- continual and intermittent reinforcement
- emotive rather than cognitive elements of a campaign
- involvement of children and young people
- reinforcement of attitudes and identity

4. Direct mail

Direct mail is regarded by marketers as an effective and increasingly important means of communication. It is now the third largest form of advertising medium by expenditure, responded to in the United States by at least 85% of the population at some time (Rossiter & Percy 1987). The growing appeal of direct mail has been added to by the increasing availability and sophistication of computerised mailing lists and letter writing through commercial organisations established for this purpose. Some services offer up to 500 specialised mailing lists ranging in content from the names of older people to purchasers of a particular magazine.

Direct mail is most effective when:

- an audience can be finely targeted
- there is a need to deliver promotion offers
- the product or service is known or easy to describe
- an action consequence is the desired outcome

There are now well-recognised techniques for increasing the response to direct mail above 1%, which is the expected level. These include: adding a personalised letter with a standard form or brochure; giving street addresses and phone numbers rather than box numbers for people to respond to; offering a money-back guarantee; and including photographs or promoter's details.

Road safety: the Traffic Accident Commission campaign

If you drink, then drive, you're a bloody idiot.

TAC
Insurance

Sponsoring body: Victorian Traffic Accident Commission.

Background: While big improvements have occurred in traffic safety in recent years, the Victorian Traffic Commission in 1989 took a new direction in traffic injury interventions.

Objectives:
1. To dramatically reduce the Victorian road toll.
2. To provoke a consistent, intrusive level of community debate on road safety.

Media: Television, outdoor, promotional support at sports events.

Market: Motor vehicle drivers in general.

Message: Personal impact of being involved in a traffic crash.

Method: Advertising, publicity.

Measure: In 12 months the campaign resulted in a 30% reduction in the road toll, with 98% consumer support and an estimated saving to the community of $361 million.

Source: Advertising Federation of Australia, Casebook of the Advertising Effectiveness Awards, 1990.

Direct mail can be used in health promotion for selling health newsletters or products, promoting functions or events, distributing pamphlets or carrying out surveys.

5. Outdoor

Outdoor media (e.g. billboards, bus sides, taxi backs, painted walls) are an effective means of creating awareness and reinforcing a campaign slogan or idea. However, the location should be carefully selected to ensure exposure to the target audience. A billboard promotion at a railway station, for example, is effective in reaching work commuters and shoppers but is unlikely to be effective for housebound persons, such as older people, who do not use public transport.

Stationary outdoor locations such as billboards, if located appropriately (e.g. at railway and bus stations, on board vehicles, at traffic light intersections), allow time for processing of information and hence can be quite informative. Moving locations, on the other hand (e.g. bus sides, taxi backs), and billboards along fast-moving traffic sections, allow only brief exposure and therefore are limited to brief images or ideas.

Outdoor promotions in recent times have become more creative, with the use of halves of smashed cars protruding from billboards to promote safe driving, and billboards that move electronically to attract attention. As technology progresses, creative techniques are likely to play an even larger part in outdoor promotions.

Outdoor media are most effective where a strong, but relatively short, message is required as part of a campaign (see Sammon 1987 for a detailed description of various outdoor media).

Table 5.1
Summary of media types

	Type	Characteristics
A. ELECTRONIC	Television	Awareness, arousal, modelling and image creation role. May also be useful for skills training.
	Radio	Informative, interactive (talkback). Cost effective and useful in creating awareness, providing information.
	Video	Possibly overrated for general health promotion, but may be useful for special interest groups. Good for training.
	Computers	Useful for information transmission, database use, self-care programs.
B. PRINT	Newspapers	Long and short copy information. Material dependent on type of paper and day of week.
	Magazines	Wide readership and influence. Useful in a supportive role and to inform and provide 'social proof'.
	Pamphlets	Information transmission. Best where cognition rather than emotion is desired.
	Information sheets	Quick, convenient information. Use as series with storage folder. Not for complex behaviour change.
	Newsletters	Continuity. Personalised. Labour-intensive and require detailed commitment and assessment of needs.
	Posters	Agenda setting function. Visual message. Creative input required.
	T-shirts	Emotive. Personal. Useful for cementing attitudes and commitment to program/idea.
	Stickers	Short messages to identify/motivate the user and cement commitment. Cheap, pervasive.
C. DIRECT MAIL		Relatively cheap and widespread where targeting is available and an action consequence is a desired outcome.

Selecting the right medium

In selecting the media to be used in any communication campaign there are a number of factors that need to be considered (e.g. see Bogart 1990; Rossiter & Percy 1987). Some of these include the following:

1. *Selectivity*, or the ability to reach a particular target audience. Magazines may be more selective in reaching specific target audiences than newspapers.

2. *Coverage*, or the penetration of a medium into a target market. A newspaper with a circulation of 500 000 in a population of two million would have a coverage of 25%.

3. *Flexibility* relates to the speed and ease with which a promotion, story, feature or advertisement can be placed in a medium, then changed, deleted or rescheduled. Radio, for example, generally has greater flexibility than other media.

4. *Costs* can be defined in absolute or relative terms. Absolute cost refers to the total outlay for the use of a medium. Paid media costs are usually described in terms of costs per thousand (or cpt), which means the cost of reaching one thousand members of the defined target audience. Relative cost is one of the main arguments for use of the mass media in health promotion.

5. *Editorial support* refers to the nature of the support that a promotion can get from editorial services in a medium. If this is forthcoming it can help to extend the promotional dollar considerably, and therefore should be taken into account in budgeting.

6. *Permanence* denotes how long a promotion is kept in front of a target audience. Permanence has to be weighed up against all other factors—including penetration, potency and affordability—to get an idea of the total impact of a medium. Ads or features in television program magazines, for example, have a far greater duration than a feature in a daily newspaper.

The Market

A COMMON MISCONCEPTION, even amongst health promotion professionals, is that media-based programs can be all things to all people and that, when disseminated among the entire population, reach everyone. There are few issues for which this is so. In fact, as society grows and changes, it becomes more diverse and forms not only groups, but sub-groups and sub-sub-groups. Health promotion practitioners who wish to reach these groups need to know their needs, interests, attitudes and beliefs. They also need to identify the media channels attended to by particular groups. This underscores the need to understand that there is rarely one universal market for a single message, but a variety of markets that require different programs and messages.

Segmentation is the concept of defining a market and targeting a message to ensure greater rationalisation of resources. Market segmentation involves breaking down the total market into various sub-groups defined in a way that implies some differential response to various marketing activities. For example, the sub-groups may have different needs requiring different product variations; they may be reached via different media channels; or they may respond to different advertising appeals or types of sales promotion. The criteria on which the segmentation is based must not only distinguish between the various sub-groups, but must also be useful in developing and implementing marketing or health programs for the different sub-groups. Commercial organisations spend a great deal of time and effort in carrying out segmentations of the market. A knowledge of the different segments allows companies to select and concentrate on one or other of these segments, given their resources vis-a-vis those of competitors.

The reasons for segmentation and ways in which markets are segmented are discussed in detail in the next chapter. This also includes a consideration of two pop- ular models of segmentation. Processes for developing market segments, including qualitative and quantitative methods, are considered in the 'Measures' section in Chapter 12.

6
Defining the market

O NE OF THE basic distinctions between social marketing health promotion campaigns and commercial marketing campaigns is that health promotion campaigns are usually based not on needs experienced by consumers, but on needs identified by health experts or government health authorities (Sirgy, Morris & Samli 1985). This often leads to a lack of segmentation of an audience and hence a 'scattergun' approach to delivering a message. A focus on consumer or client needs naturally calls for a segmentation of the prospective audience, as it is obvious that vastly different sub-groups exist in a population, that the differences occur on a variety of dimensions (or bases), and that different strategies and approaches are necessary to effectively reach and communicate with these different sub-groups.

Segmentation of an audience involves three phases (Kotler 1989):

1. dividing the total market into segments and developing profiles of these segments
2. evaluating each segment and selecting one or more segments as target markets
3. developing a detailed strategy for each of the selected segments

Commercial organisations utilise a great number of resources identifying and determining which segments will be most profitable for them. Taking into account competitors' activities in the various segments, selection is based primarily on a match between the company's resources and the target segment's needs, and characteristics such as size, accessibility, persuasibility, geographic location, purchasing power, and other factors that contribute to the segment's viability. For mass media-based campaigns, major selection criteria relate to whether the segments are reachable via one or more mass media channels and whether the message to be promoted can be communicated adequately by those media.

Segments can be described or profiled in many ways such as shown in Table 6.1:

For health promotion campaigns, target groups are often identified in terms of risk factors (e.g. smokers; the obese; the inactive; heavy drinkers; diabetics), or demographic groupings that epidemiologically appear at higher risk (e.g. blue collar groups; sedentary occupations; Aborigines; street kids). Regardless of the base(s) chosen for the initial segmentation (e.g. age and sex), in order that the segments can be better

Table 6.1
Some bases for target audience segmentation

Demographic	Age, sex, income, education, religion, ethnicity, occupation, family life cycle.
Geographic	State, region, city size, density (urban, suburban, rural, remote), climate, local government area, postcode, census collector's district.
Psychographic	Values, lifestyle, personality type.
Socio-demographic	Social class.
Epidemiological	Risk factor status.
Behavioural	Frequency, intensity, regularity.
Attitudinal	Positive–neutral–negative.
Benefits sought	Varies by issue (e.g. avoid disease, sensory enjoyment, peace of mind).
Readiness stage	Prochaska's stages (see below).

understood they are also defined according to as many other variables as possible. However, there is some disagreement on how the segmentation process should proceed.

One popular method in the marketing and advertising area is the psychographic or lifestyle approach. In this procedure, respondents answer a number of attitude, belief and behaviour questions (usually 50 to 100), relating to the issue in question. Multivariate methods such as factor analysis, discriminant analysis and cluster analysis are then used to develop the segments. The psychographic approach has appeal because it generates segments more richly described than the traditional demographic segment descriptions of, for example, 'married, 2.5 children, aged 30–45, lower-middle socio-economic level'. Psychographic segments list descriptions such as 'outgoing, active in community activities, enjoys physical activities rather than reading, prefers barbecues rather than dinner parties', and are given catchy segment titles such as 'swinging singles', 'elderly adventurers' or 'new-age sensitive man'.

Some health researchers have segmented on the basis of attitudes to health issues. For example, Slater and Flora (1989) cluster analysed respondents' answers to a large number of health belief, attitude and behaviour items; measures of social influence with respect to health issues; and demographics. They identified seven clusters (or segments) which were found to differ significantly with respect to various risk factors such as smoking and alcohol consumption. The implication is that segments with high proportions of at-risk persons should be targeted using a knowledge of that *total* segment's beliefs and attitudes with respect to these risk factors and other health issues.

This approach has been criticised (e.g. see Rossiter 1989) as *'backward' segmentation*. The problem is that, for an audience segment such as smokers, strategies are developed on the beliefs and attitudes of the total segment, rather than on the beliefs and attitudes of only the smokers in the segment. A more direct and efficient approach would be to segment *all* smokers on the basis of their attitudes and beliefs to smoking, and then target strategies towards these different sub-groups based on each sub-group's beliefs and attitudes with respect to smoking.

Rossiter (1989) argues that because the objectives for any communication campaign are to change beliefs and/or attitudes and ultimately, behaviour, overall segmentation must be in terms of these two dimensions. For example, smokers could be segmented behaviourally by amount smoked (e.g. heavy, medium and light) and attitudinally by beliefs and attitudes towards quitting, as in Table 6.2.

Table 6.2
Segmentation by smoking behaviour and attitudes to quitting

| | | Attitude to quitting | | |
		Positive	Neutral	Negative
AMOUNT SMOKED	Heavy > 25 cigs./day			
	Medium 11–24 cigs./day			
	Light 10 or less per day			

In Rossiter's terms, selected target segments can then be profiled demographically (to assist in media selection), and psychographically (to assist in message language and style). That is, demographics and psychographics should be used in a *descriptive* and not in a *prescriptive* manner.

Sheth and Frazier (1982) present a similar attitude–behaviour segmentation (see Table 6.3). They provide a systematic procedure not only for describing various target segments in terms of attitude and behaviour (i.e. the 'diagnosis'), but also suggest a strategy for achieving behaviour change within each of the defined segments (i.e. the 'prognosis'). For example, Segment 1 requires a *reinforcement* strategy, Segment 4 an *incentive* strategy, and Segment 6 a *confrontational* strategy. The nature of the segments also allows a determination of whether or not mass media messages are an appropriate and cost-effective method for influencing the different segments. For example, Segments 4 and 5 are far more likely than Segment 6 to respond to a media campaign, and Segment 6 probably requires a totally different approach. However, even in this case, mass media may be used to increase that target group's awareness of the issue. In short, the media will play different roles in campaigns directed toward the different segments.

Table 6.3
Sheth–Frazier segmentation model

Behaviour	Attitude to behaviour		
	POSITIVE	NEUTRAL	NEGATIVE
Perform desired behaviour	1	2	3
Do not perform desired behaviour	4	5	6

Large-scale surveys are necessary to determine the proportions of the total population falling into each of the segments. To assist in determining which segments of the audience should be concentrated on, these are profiled in terms of their demographics, media habits, lifestyle variables, risk factor profiles and other relevant health beliefs and attitudes.

Target market and target audience selection: the TARPAR approach

GIVEN THE APPROACH to segmentation provided by Sheth and Frazier as shown above, a number of procedures are available for determining the appropriate selection of segments for targeting. Donovan (Donovan 1987; Donovan & Owen 1993) suggest the following criteria:

1. The *T*otal number of persons in that category: in general, the more people in a category, the higher the priority of that category.
2. The proportion in that category classed as '*At R*isk' (high or moderate): (i.e. those whose behaviour, if modified, would provide the greatest reduction in health costs). In general, the greater this proportion, the potentially greater 'return', and hence the higher the category's priority.
3. The *P*ersuasibility of the target audience: (i.e. the extent to which members of the target audience are amenable to being convinced to alter their behaviour). In general, the more amenable, the more likely a media campaign can be cost effective, and the higher the priority.
4. The *A*ccessibility of the target audience: (i.e. the extent to which the target audience expose themselves to available media). The more accessible the target audience, the more likely an effective outcome and the higher the priority. This measure should take into account 'cost per thousand' data. For example, a target audience may be accessible, but the necessary media may be expensive.
5. Additional *R*esources necessary to meet the needs of the target audience: (i.e. the extent to which each target segment can be induced to accept the recommended behaviour, given current services and facilities). Various target audi-

ences might be motivated to engage in particular activities by a mass media campaign, but it may require new programs or facilities to meet this demand.

These factors can be subsumed in the following formula:

Priority = $F(w_1T, w_2AR, w_3P, w_4A, w_5R)$, where

w represents weights attached to the various factors.

T = total number in segment

AR = % at (high) risk

P = persuasibility

A = accessibility

R = additional resources required

T and AR can be measured objectively, P requires a subjective estimate based on attitudinal research, A requires media exposure research, and R requires an analysis of existing resources and a survey of consumer preferences amongst the target audience. These factors can be measured quantitatively through surveys and questionnaires, or qualitatively through such processes as focus groups (see Chapter 12).

It should be noted that the above selection formula is only a guide to segment selection. In many situations, local issues and social justice factors must also be taken into account. For example, groups consisting of people with disabilities or Aborigines are very small in absolute numbers, and hence could be overlooked if a standard 'mathematical' procedure were used to select target audiences. Similarly, in times of crisis (e.g. infectious disease outbreaks), resources are naturally directed as the local situation requires.

Another distinction to be made is that between target *audiences* and target *markets* or *segments*. The target market constitutes all members included in the definition of that market, whereas the target audience consists of those members of the target market who are accessible via available media. A target market or segment therefore refers to all individuals to be targeted by a program *in its entirety*. The target audience(s) refer to those individuals to be targeted by the *media* components of the program—whether or not they are also subject to other program elements. For example, urban Aborigines might be defined as the target segment for a late onset diabetes campaign consisting of a number of community-based actions and some television advertising and publicity. In this case, only those with access to a television, and who are likely to watch it, would constitute the target audience for the media component of the campaign.

A staged approach to segmentation: the Prochaska model

A SEGMENTATION MODEL for health promotion derives from James Prochaska's clinical work with cigarette and drug addiction (Prochaska 1991.) Prochaska divides the total target segment (e.g. all females at risk of breast cancer), into sub-segments depending on their stage in progression toward adoption of the desired behaviour (i.e. self-exam-

Table 6.4
Segmenting for exercise

An example of the Sheth–Frazier approach to segmentation is shown in this table of attitudes and beliefs about exercise. Qualitative research was undertaken to determine the parameters of each segment. These data were used to identify those segments most likely to respond to a media-based strategy and to determine what should be the content and execution of the media messages.

| | Overall valence of attitudes and beliefs about exercise | | |
| | | | |
Exercise behaviour	POSITIVE	NEGATIVE or NEUTRAL	TOTAL
Exercise at or near level for cardiovascular benefits	11%	3%	14%
Light–moderate exercise sufficient for some cardiovascular benefits	35%	19%	54%
No exercise (sedentary)	16%	16%	32%
TOTAL	62%	38%	100%

Source: Donovan 1989.

ination for breast cancer). Prochaska's concept is similar to marketing's 'buyer readiness' segmentation, which states that at any particular point in time the market can be described in terms of those unaware of the product, those aware of the product, those informed about the product, those interested in the product, those motivated to buy the product, and those who have formed an intention to buy the product (Kotler 1989). The implications of this are that marketing objectives and strategy will vary according to the relative proportions of the total market in each of these different stages.

Prochaska's stages are:

1. *Precontemplation*—where the individual is not even considering modifying his or her unhealthy behaviour.
2. *Contemplation*—where the individual is considering changing an unhealthy behaviour, but not in the immediate future.
3. *Preparation*—where the individual plans to try to change the unhealthy behaviour in the immediate future (i.e. in the next two weeks).
4. *Action*—the immediate (six month) period following trial and adoption of the recommended behaviour and cessation of the unhealthy behaviour.
5. *Maintenance*—the period following the action stage until the unhealthy behaviour is fully extinguished.

6. *Termination*—when the problem behaviour is completely eliminated, that is, 'zero temptation across all problem situations' (Prochaska 1991, page 806).

Donovan and Owen (1993) claim that mass media health promotion campaigns are most influential in the precontemplation and contemplation stages (by raising the salience and personal relevance of the issue), of moderate influence in the preparation stage (by reinforcing perceptions of self-efficacy and maintaining salience of the perceived benefits of adopting the recommended behaviour), and of least influence in the action and maintenance stages where beliefs and attitudes are well established and where socio-environmental influences on the achieved behaviour are greatest (see Table 6.5).

Table 6.5
Prochaska's stages and proposed relative influence of mass media campaigns

PROCHASKA STAGES	CAMPAIGN COMMUNICATION OBJECTIVES	BEHAVIOURAL (INTENTION) OBJECTIVES	MASS MEDIA INFLUENCE
Precontemplation	Raise awareness of issues, personal relevance	Seek further information	High
Contemplation	Increase personal relevance; build response efficacy	Form an intention to try	Moderate–high
Preparation	Build self-efficacy; reinforce reasons for trial	Trial	Moderate
Action	Reinforce reasons for adoption; maintain motivational and efficacy support	Adoption	Low
Maintenance	Maintain reasons for adoption	Maintain new behaviour	Low

Usual methods of target audience selection

TARGET AUDIENCES FOR campaigns are usually selected as follows:
1. Epidemiological data are used to determine what 'diseases' are to be targeted.
2. One or more risk factors associated with the selected 'disease' are then chosen for targeting.
3. Epidemiological data are then used to identify demographic groups (including geographic and socio-economic groups in particular), or lifecycle/lifestyle groups who are disproportionately represented in the mortality, morbidity or risk factor data.

4. Qualitative research is used to determine the attitudes, beliefs and behaviours within the target groups, and quantitative research is used to determine what percentages of the target groups hold the particular beliefs and attitudes.
5. The selected target segments are then defined in terms of actual risk behaviours, and attitudes towards adopting the alternate healthy behaviour(s).

The final target audience(s) should then be described as completely as possible to aid in:

- *locating* the audience(s)
- *communicating* with the target audience(s)
- *motivating* the target audience(s)

In the absence of comprehensive information about the media habits of the target audience(s)—which would allow direct matching of target audience to media vehicles—demographics are used to *locate* the target audience(s); lifestyle, social class and 'psychographics' are used to ensure that appropriate symbols, language and values are used in messages to enhance *communicating* with the target audience(s); and an understanding of beliefs, attitudes and motives underlying current behaviours is used to *motivate* the target audience(s).

'Hard-to-reach' audiences

SOME CRITICISM OF the use of mass media has centred on the claim that mass media are ineffective in reaching important target groups. In some cases this is a valid criticism, in that media campaigns have been directed toward various groups that would have been more effectively targeted via some other methods. The question remains, whether the media can be used to reach 'hard-to-reach' (HTR) groups, and, if so, what roles would they play for these groups?

Hard-to-reach groups are usually defined in terms of their non-responsiveness to mainstream media campaigns. However, it is important to distinguish between those who are hard-to-reach because of: (a) low access to mainstream media; and (b) those who are hard to reach because of apparent imperviousness to media campaigns. The latter definition is the one most commonly used (e.g. White & Maloney 1990), and accessibility is often included as a correlate of personality and lifestyle factors such as a distrust of large government organisations, a sense of fatalism, and poor cognitive processing skills (Freimuth & Mettger 1990). We suggest two alternative definitions: (a) 'hard-to-reach' refers to those not accessible via media; and (b) 'hard-to-impact' refers to those not responsive to media-delivered messages.

Groups like prostitutes, IV drug users, street kids and other homeless persons, Aboriginal fringe dwellers, and non-English speaking migrants are generally thought of with respect to accessibility. Yet there is now considerable evidence that such groups are accessible via mainstream media, including ethnic media, although care must be taken in scheduling and vehicle selection (Donovan et al. 1991; Bednall 1992; Research

Triangle Institute 1990). With respect to both accessibility and responsiveness, the answer lies in carrying out adequate formative research to assess whether or not a potential target audience is firstly accessible and then, given accessibility, whether it is likely to be responsive to media messages. In some cases, the role of media may be limited to directing people to other campaign interventions (e.g. telephone information services; interpreter services; needle exchange locations), rather than to belief or attitude change.

Summary

BOTH OF THE models described here provide a format for determining a number of audience segments. Segment sizes and characteristics can then be determined through a number of different techniques ranging from 'guesstimates' based on knowledge and experience to more-structured qualitative and/or quantitative research. Market research techniques such as literature searches, focus groups, questionnaires and survey samples can be used at this phase of a campaign to help understand target segments.

The Message

MESSAGE REFERS TO the development of communications that, when appropriately processed by a target audience, will produce the beliefs and attitudes that are necessary to achieve the desired behavioural outcome. Message strategy is possibly the most crucial of the five Ms. Getting the right message is a necessary condition for success, but it is not a sufficient condition. Astute selection of media, proper targeting and use of sophisticated media methods are required for overall campaign effectiveness.

It is important not only to *get the right message*, but also to *get the message right*. The way in which the message is executed for the target audience will largely determine its effectiveness (given that it has the potential to be effective in the first place) with that target audience.

Getting the right message is the responsibility of the health promotion professional in conjunction with social researchers experienced in the health communications field. This requires a knowledge of scientific evidence and how the target audience will respond to various aspects of the evidence. The fact that chlamydia has serious consequences for female reproduction, may be the 'right message' to persuade non-monogamous, sexually active young females to use condoms for casual sexual contacts. However, this needs to be expressed in a language and style that the target market (e.g. 16–24-year-old females) can accept and are motivated to act upon. In other words, the message needs to be made 'right'.

The responsibility for *getting the message right* should, whenever possible, be given to suitably skilled wordsmiths and image makers. For press releases, a public relations journalist and photographer are the appropriate persons; for advertising, it is the role of the copywriter and art director to execute the message. In all of these cases it is essential that health professionals and behavioural scientists work closely with these communicators to ensure that the execution retains the original message strategy. Apart from expert eyeballing of the execution, pretesting should ensure that the execution communicates the desired message.

In Chapter 7, we look at the processes of determining the right message. This includes research and measurement techniques, some of which are dealt with in more detail in Chapter 12. In Chapter 8, we look at getting the message right, and particularly at those processes in the development of media materials that can help to finetune a message for a specific role.

7

Getting the right message

HAVING SELECTED A target audience and a set of behavioural objectives, determining the right message involves identifying the kinds of beliefs and attitudes that need to be reinforced, created or changed, and the kinds of motives that need to be aroused so as to bring about the desired behaviour changes. That is, determining the right message begins with a clear understanding of the campaign's objectives. Often, in both the health and the commercial areas, the message strategy is driven by creative ideas instead of by clearly defined communication objectives that should be the driving force. Campaigns have specific, as well as overall objectives, and many campaigns have multiple objectives aimed at different target audiences. This should be recognised when developing messages—many health professionals try to achieve too many objectives and/or reach too many audiences with the one message.

In this chapter we look first at a number of overall campaign communication objectives, then focus on establishing the specific communication objectives for a campaign.

Broad communication objectives

THE BROAD ROLES or objectives for the media, whether via advertising, publicity or edutainment, are listed below (see Donovan & Robinson 1992; Flora, Maibach & Maccoby 1989). These are classified under the three overall roles of informing, persuading or advocating. However, it should be noted that the classification is not a mutually exclusive one.

Information objectives
- *Informing* (or educating) people about the negative health effects of various unhealthy behaviours, and the positive health effects of alternative behaviours.
- *Clarifying* misperceptions and/or confusions that people may have about various health issues.

- *Reminding* people of the positive and negative health effects of which they are already aware and maintaining the impact of this knowledge.

Motivation or persuasion objectives

- *Reinforcing* those already practising healthy lifestyle behaviours.
- Generating *emotional arousal* to increase people's motivations to cease unhealthy practices and/or to adopt various health practices.
- *Sensitising* or predisposing individuals to other contributory influences (arguably the major role as a facilitator of behaviour change).
- Increasing awareness of both prescriptive and, where appropriate, popular *norms* (Cialdini 1989), and hence providing social support for those who wish to adopt the recommended behaviour.
- Stimulating *word-of-mouth* communications about the issue in question and hence encouraging peer (and other) group discussion and decision making—a very important role for the diffusion of social issues (Rogers 1983).

Advocacy-related objectives

- *Increasing community awareness* of a health issue—that is, placing the issue on the community's agenda or 'agenda setting' (Ghorpade 1986).
- Creating or increasing community awareness of a particular point of view with respect to an issue—that is, '*framing*' the community agenda.
- *Creating or maintaining a favourable attitude* towards this particular view.
- Creating a view that the issue is a significantly serious one for community concern—that is, '*legitimising*' the issue.
- Generating a positive *community mood* within which health authority policies (including research and regulatory measures) can be introduced with minimal opposition and/or maximal support.

Public announcement objectives

- *Directing* people to information on where and how to get help or 'how to help oneself '.
- *Informing* the target audience of *specific events* ('June 15 is Quit Day'), or programs and services ('Aerobics classes, 3 pm daily, St Bernhard's Hall').

All of these are general objectives. The next step is to set specific objectives with respect to 'time' and 'amount' for the selected target audiences for the campaign. For example:

- to increase awareness of the HIV/AIDS hotline amongst 18–25-year-old men who have sex with men, from 22% to 50% by the end of the campaign
- to increase the proportion of the public who feel they can influence public health policy, from 10% to 15% in the first three months of the campaign

- to reduce the prevalence of smoking among 18–25-year-old women in unskilled occupations, from 35% to 30% in one year

Given these specific objectives, determining the message begins with an attempt to understand the beliefs and attitudes the target audiences hold that support their unhealthy behaviours, the changes necessary to induce cessation of these unhealthy behaviours, what 'new' information might influence change, what benefits might motivate the desired change, and what socio-structural facilitators and inhibitors might have to be dealt with in the message strategy. At this stage, an understanding of Knowledge–Attitude–Behaviour change models (KAB models) is helpful in developing the message strategy.

Using KAB models as a guide

KNOWLEDGE–ATTITUDE–BEHAVIOUR (KAB) models exist in a number of forms that are relevant to developing messages for media campaigns: Fishbein's theory of reasoned action (Fishbein & Ajzen 1975); Rogers' protection motivation theory (1975; 1983); Festinger's dissonance theory (1957); Bandura's social learning theory (1977; 1986); the health belief model (Janz & Becker 1984), and the theory of trying (Bagozzi & Warshaw 1990). Several of these are summarised in Egger, Spark and Lawson (1990).

There is much overlap between these models and attempts have been made to compare and combine some of them. For example, Cummings, Becker and Maile (1980) had a panel of experts sort 109 variables from 14 models into groups, based on the similarity of the variables. Smallest Space Analysis (a form of multidimensional scaling) revealed six interpretable factors:

1. Accessibility to health care (e.g. affordability, awareness of services, location convenience).
2. Evaluation of health care (e.g. beliefs about quality of treatment and benefits of treatment).
3. Perceptions of the threat of illness (e.g. susceptibility, severity, symptoms).
4. Knowledge about disease (i.e. awareness of facts about disease).
5. Social network characteristics (i.e. social norms, social interactions).
6. Demographic characteristics (including social status).

The main point to note from these models is that most begin with beliefs as the basis for attitude and behaviour change, and hence most strategies attempt to:

- change beliefs (e.g. increase the perceived likelihood of contracting chlamydia)
- change the evaluation of beliefs (e.g. increase the perceived severity of the consequences of contracting chlamydia by increasing knowledge or salience of the potential infertility effects of chlamydia)
- introduce new relevant beliefs (e.g. having chlamydia increases susceptibility to the AIDS virus).

These KAB models apply equally to beliefs and attitudes about health behaviours and to beliefs and attitudes about the social and political issues related to those health behaviours. Hence they are useful not only for developing campaigns to promote healthy behaviours, but also for developing advocacy campaigns.

Eat less fat

Sponsoring body: WA Department of Health.

Background: Fat makes up about 35% of the Australian diet, compared to the recommended 30%. This is responsible for a range of diseases from heart disease to certain cancers.

Objectives:
1. Increase awareness of the risks of dietary fat intake.
2. Increase knowledge about three ways of reducing fat ('take the skin off the chook'; 'ease the spread on the bread'; 'forget the dob when you cook').

Media: TV, radio; brochures, pamphlets, fact sheets, and a low fat cookbook through newsagents; cooking demonstrations; competitions.

Market: Primary: food purchasers and preparers. Secondary: general public.

Message: Reduce dietary fat for increased health. Slogan: 'Eat less fat'.

Method: Advertising; publicity.

Measures: 89% awareness of at least one suggested change. There were also changes in dietary behaviour after one year with between 6–9% increases in use of low fat cheeses, milk, sandwich spreads and removal of chicken skins. Over 50 000 copies of a cookbook *Flavour Without Fat* were sold.

Source: Coli 1990.

There is a broad variety of beliefs that need to be taken into account when developing messages. Our synthesis of the KAB models suggests that the following are the key variables to research and to consider incorporating in message strategy for an *individual change* campaign.

Assume a target audience 'at risk' for heart disease:

1. What are individuals' PERCEIVED LIKELIHOOD of contracting heart disease, given no change in their current behaviour?

- What beliefs or perceptions underlie this perceived likelihood?
- If the perceived likelihood is unrealistically low, what sort of information, presented in what way, and by whom, might increase this likelihood?

2. How do individuals PERCEIVE the SEVERITY of the consequences of contracting heart disease? Is this realistic? If not, what sort of information, presented in what way and by whom might change this perception?

3. What are individuals' ATTITUDES toward adopting the recommended alternative behaviours such as a change in diet or adoption of exercise? Are some behaviours more acceptable than others? Why?
   - What are the PERCEIVED BENEFITS of continuing the risk behaviours?
   - What are the perceived benefits and the DISBENEFITS of the alternative behaviours?
   - What social and physical barriers inhibit adoption of the recommended behaviours? What facilitators exist?

4. How do individuals PERCEIVE THE LIKELIHOOD OF AVERTING THE THREAT if the recommended behaviours are adopted?
   - If it is thought that there is little likelihood, on what beliefs is this perception based?
   - What information might change this perception?

5. What are individuals' beliefs about their ABILITY TO ADOPT THE RECOMMENDED BEHAVIOURS?
   - On what beliefs are these perceptions of ability based?
   - Is skills training required?
   - What intermediate goals can be set to induce trial?

6. What appear to be the MAJOR MOTIVATIONS THAT WOULD INDUCE TRIAL?
   - Are positive benefits (e.g. feeling well, increased capacity for physical activity) more motivating than negative benefits (e.g. avoidance of disease) for some individuals or groups, and vice versa for others?

7. What are the individuals' main SOURCES OF INFORMATION on health?
   - Who are the major influencers?
   - Who might be additional credible sources of information and influence?

8. How do individuals' SOCIAL INTERACTIONS—including extended family, club memberships, employment and home-care role—influence health beliefs and behaviours?

9. Do the individuals exhibit any PERSONALITY characteristics that might inhibit or facilitate the adoption of healthy behaviours?

Research that seeks to answer the above questions is called 'formative' research because it helps to develop or 'form' the strategy for the campaign. How these answers are obtained is dealt with below. Answering the above questions helps to both finetune, or even determine, the communication objectives for the campaign (i.e. various information gaps or misperceptions may be discovered) and to develop the message strategy (i.e. determine what information would be most effective in influencing behaviour or attitudes). For example, early anti-smoking campaigns focused on lung cancer as a deterrent and fear of contracting it as a stimulus for quitting. Later research showed that a belief that smoking was related to heart disease also was a significant stimulus for quitting for many smokers. Quit campaigns then began to include heart disease messages. Even later research showed that while the threat of lung cancer was 'wearing out' in terms of its influence on hard-core smokers, the threat of throat cancer was a powerful stimulus to quit. Testimonial advertising showing ex-smokers who had a tracheostomy because of tobacco-induced throat cancer then became a feature of quit campaigns.

Methods for message determination

A VARIETY OF different qualitative and quantitative research techniques are available for determining the right message. Ideally, the process would consist of these methods:

1. Literature and background review

This can take the form of a library search, computer database search, analysis of previous campaigns in the same field and interviews with experts. The research provides a general understanding of the area, highlighting various issues and identifying hypotheses for testing in primary or contact research. A study of what has, and has not, worked in previous campaigns is particularly useful.

2. Qualitative research

In commercial marketing research, there is a belief that: '. . . qualitative research is the only research method capable of—and we stress capable of, not assured of—discovering the causes of buyer behavior' (Rossiter & Percy 1987).

Qualitative research generally consists of 'focus groups' or informal or semi-formal individual in-depth interviews. Qualitative research should not be confused with quantitative analysis where conclusions are drawn on the basis of proportions of the population from sample statistics.

Qualitative research is concerned with discovering, describing and attempting to probe the determinants of the various points of view that exist in a selected target audience. Qualitative research attempts to understand how these were developed, the interrelationships between various beliefs, attitudes and behaviour, and what motivations underlie behaviour. Such an understanding provides 'clues' as to what message strategy would be appropriate to reinforce, create or alter attitudes and behaviours. Message strategy development is therefore an iterative process where the researcher is constantly developing and testing hypotheses against the target group—both within an interview situation and in a series of interview situations.

The validity of qualitative research findings is largely determined by the skill of the interviewer. Hence it is essential that properly trained in-depth interviewers or focus group moderators be used in order to gain benefit from the research and to avoid incorrect message strategies that are based on misinterpretation of qualitative data. For a detailed description of focus groups in formative as well as evaluative research, see Chapter 12.

3. Ethnographic or observational research

Discreet observer and participant observer techniques are increasingly being borrowed from anthropology and sociology to increase our understanding of behaviour and its influencers. These kinds of techniques range from rubbish analysis, to hidden cameras observing TV audience behaviour, to street gang participation. In many cases though, it simply means objectively observing the behaviour under study, attempting to construct behaviour patterns, and making inferences about the relationships between beliefs, attitudes, motives and behaviour. Observational methods are particularly useful for studying the influence of social factors on behaviour.

These methods are used in conjunction with individual or focus group interviews to further probe the relationships noted above.

'Situation spotting' for message content—random breath testing

The introduction of random breath testing in NSW involved focus groups with the target audience (drinkers and drivers) which concluded that appeals to responsibility and concerns for safety were insufficient motivation for drinkers to avoid driving, but that a more personalised approach involving embarrassment could be effective. By spending several nights situation 'spotting' with police traffic patrols, a skilled advertising copywriter was able to tap the parameters of this embarrassment by observing the humiliation of otherwise self-respecting business and family men—average people—when placed in a police dock and having tie, shoe laces etc. removed.
The resultant campaign, based around the slogan and jingle

How will you go when you sit for the test? Will you be under .05 or under arrest?

utilised this embarrassment by showing the discomfort of 'average citizens' in this situation in a television advertisement.

---

4. Quantitative research

Quantitative research (e.g. field surveys of representative samples) attempts to determine what proportion of the population hold certain points of view. Hence, survey research is often carried out to determine the necessity of dealing with various issues by determining the population percentages that hold, for example, misperceptions about the issue. Survey data also can be used to look at the interrelationships between beliefs, attitudes and behaviour suggested by the qualitative research. For example, correlation analysis might reveal that those who believe that there is a quick and easy cure for chlamydia are those least likely to believe that condoms should be used for casual sexual encounters.

Overall then, sample surveys can be used to assess size of demographic (geographic) and psychographic aspects of a target audience relevant to the intervention. Surveys can also be used to measure media exposure, population distributions of influencing factors and other aspects of a campaign which need population statistics. Survey research in the formative stages in health promotion may be used to gather baseline data for evaluation of an intervention.

Having determined what is the right message, various communication objectives, along with the necessary supporting material, can then be presented to advertising copywriters for the development of ads; to public relations consultants for the development of press releases, feature articles and briefing notes for health professionals for media interviews; and to entertainment script writers for incorporation into programming. Where multiple methods are used, it is necessary to ensure that all media components are consistent in their content, style, language and tone. (Of course not all of these media methods will be available for every campaign and the communication objectives will vary by method used.)

The responsibility of the above media professionals (or do-it-yourself health professionals) is to 'get the message right'. This is dealt with in the next chapter.

8

Getting the message right

The features, quality, styling, brand name and packaging
of each of these . . . [messages] . . . can have a far reaching impact.
(Lefebvre & Flora 1988)

THIS CHAPTER defines what we mean by 'getting the message right', then looks more deeply at specific aspects of preparation that can increase the potency and effectiveness of a message within the print and electronic media. Some parameters of print that we look at are writing style, print type and graphics. The variables in TV and radio are the use of a presenter, use of music, graphics versus print, 'voice-overs', ad placement and 'action tags'.

Although a lot has been written about each of these, there has been no concerted attempt to extrapolate the findings from commercial advertising, journalism or public relations to health promotion and public health. Each requires a book in itself. Hence only the most important parameters are considered here.

What we mean by 'getting the message right'

ONCE THE COMMUNICATION objectives for a campaign are decided upon, and the media methods are chosen, the actual communication materials have to be constructed. For example, if the campaign is to involve advertising, the actual ads have to be written and produced; if the campaign involves publicity, press releases and feature articles have to be written, illustrated, and produced. Getting the message right refers to:

1. The materials being produced in a language, style and tone that are consistent, not only with the message objectives, but also suited to the target audience's background and lifestyle.
2. The correct or accurate translation of the communication objectives into the communication materials, so that the message is understood, accepted and appropriately motivating to the target audience.

A press release or feature article needs to express the concept decided on in the strategy development phase. In this sense, the concept is the 'angle' that the article will take on the issue. For example, after research showed that many young people believe that they can identify persons likely to be STD infected by their looks, the concept (or strategy) chosen for a STD/HIV campaign would be to convince the target audience that 'you can't tell by looking'. This theme should then be the major focus of press releases and feature articles for the campaign. Furthermore, press releases attempting to translate scientific findings need to ensure that the findings are accurately portrayed and in a language that the target audience can understand and relate to.

Brochures targeted at teenagers should, as far as possible, use symbols, language and music popular with teenagers. In fact, 'brochures' for some target audiences (e.g. prisoners, young children, homeless IV drug users), have been presented as comics that are visually appealing and that require minimal literacy.

For advertising, there is usually a vast variety of alternative executions for a particular communication objective. An ad dealing with the STD concept (above) could be presented in a variety of ways, limited only by the creativity of the copywriter. Pretesting is therefore carried out not only to determine whether the executions are understandable, acceptable and motivating to the target audiences, but also to determine which of the forms of presentation is most effective.

Message testing

Message testing occurs after copy content has been developed. The aim here is to confirm the understandability, credibility, impact and relevance of the copy content before going to the expense of final production. With print messages (i.e. ads, press releases, brochures, articles), rough art or simply typed statements can be used to test the message. With radio (advertising, news items), a rough recording or draft script can be used. With television advertising, either *story boards* or *animatics* are the usual form for testing.

Story boards represent the television action in draft art form on a series of large boards or placards. A presenter then talks through the action with the viewer, or this is presented on tape. With *animatics*, the story board action is filmed as a sequence of stills on video with a draft voice-over intended to accompany the final version.

Focus groups are often used for message testing, but there are good reasons why these are not appropriate, including interpersonal influences, cost and inappropriate processing conditions (Rossiter & Donovan 1983). A better form of testing is individual interviews which are carried out face to face. Single prepared messages are presented to an individual (e.g. in shopping centres) and structured questions are asked about that message. If information is the basis of the exposure, pre- and post-exposure questions can be asked in order to assess information gain. The point is that, at this stage of message development, quantitative data are required to make a 'go–no-go' decision on whether to release the materials. For example, if an ad is correctly understood by only 65% of the target audience sample, the recommendation would be to re-do the ad. Qualitative research—such as focus groups—cannot provide such data. Given that the cost of media placement is the major expense in advertising campaigns, if 35% do not understand the ad, 35% of the media dollars is being wasted.

Issues in print

PRINT IS A visual medium with two main components—words and pictures. Words are the raw materials of writers and journalists; pictures are the tools of artists and photographers. Graphic designers combine words and pictures in the most effective way.

Writing

Contrary to popular opinion, publications that are more easily understood are often the hardest in which to get accurate health information across. For example, it is often harder to simplify medical research results accurately for the daily press than to write about these, without simplification, for medical or scientific journals. Because of the need for accuracy, scientific writing often tends to be qualified—the opposite of what is required for general readership.

For these reasons, scientists and medical practitioners are often not the best people to write health promotion material. Journalists, on the other hand, will often not have the scientific or medical knowledge to properly 'translate' scientific information. The health promotion practitioner, working with the media, can therefore complement his or her health knowledge with good writing skills.

There are a number of characteristics of good writing which can, and should, be applied to health promotion material. These are:

(a) Brevity

If an idea can be expressed simply, there is no excuse for making it complicated. This relates in particular to length and number of words. In general, if a short word can be used instead of a long one (e.g. 'cheap' instead of 'inexpensive'), use it; if one word can be substituted for a phrase (e.g. 'consider' instead of 'give consideration to'), substitute it. Say Strunk and White (1971):

> Vigorous writing is concise. A sentence should contain no unnecessary words, a paragraph no unnecessary sentences, for the same reason that a drawing should have no unnecessary lines and a machine no unnecessary parts.

The most obvious sign of bureaucracy in a health communication is verbosity. Depending on the target group and the topic, written copy in health promotion may need to be either long (e.g. nutrition education to an educated audience) or short (e.g. anti-smoking promotions to current smokers). Either way, copy length should not be confused with brevity. Short, informative sentences hold attention more than long, drawn out rambling connections of words.

The booklet as information

A booklet, as the name implies, is a cross between a pamphlet and a book. As such, it has value for anyone who requires a reasonable amount of information about a topic of interest, but may not want to go into it in exhaustive detail. A booklet is usually in demand by a 'ready made' target audience, and although it should have visual appeal to encourage usage, the visual style can be quite different from motivational media, such as posters. In terms of our previous classification, booklets are designed to provide 'light', not 'heat'.

Some basic rules for brevity include the following (Acquaviva & Malone 1981):

- *Avoid 'padding'.* Excessive words or sentences are an indication that the writer is unsure about expressing an idea.
- *Avoid adverbial 'dressing gowns'.* Adverbs are used excessively, according to Gowers (1954), '. . . as if they [the adjectives] were indecent and must have an adverbial dressing gown thrown around them'. The phrase 'it is a serious disease' is cluttered up by the use of an adverb—for example, 'it is a terribly serious disease'.
- *Avoid lofty leads.* Brevity is exemplified by avoiding lofty introductions. 'It is interesting to note that . . . ' or 'It is important to bear in mind that . . . ' can almost always be discarded and the sentence started with whatever follows the word 'that'.

- *Avoid tautology.* The unnecessary repetition of words is often, but not always, obvious. To 'repeat again . . .' may seem an obvious tautology. A 'square-shaped object' may not. Both use words excessively.
- *Avoid diluting verbs.* 'To make a study of . . . ' can be just as forcefully expressed as '. . . to study'; to be ' . . . found in agreement with each other . . . ' is much better written as ' . . . to agree'. The dilution of verbs is a common practice in scientific writing.

(b) Positiveness

It is usually better to be positive than negative, but in health promotion—a discipline fraught with negativeness—positiveness is even more important. Hence, while it may be scientifically prudent to say ' . . . there is no evidence to suggest that a low fat diet is not beneficial to health . . . ', a more effective, albeit less-cautious approach is: '. . . *a low fat diet is healthy*'.

(c) Clarity

Clarity is the essence of health promotion 'translation': 'I think that the fear of being understood and held accountable for what we say drives many of us to great lengths to be obscure.' (Acquaviva & Malone 1981). Nowhere is this more so than in scientific journalism. The use of jargon and superfluous words is, as the nineteenth century novelist, Herman Melville, pointed out, for the ' . . . smatterer in science who thinks that by mouthing hard words he proves that he understands hard things' (Acquaviva & Malone 1981, page 21).

Clarity and brevity are related by some simple rules such as:

- always choosing the familiar rather than the obscure word
- never using two words when one will do
- leaving out what is in doubt

(d) Style

Style is the personality or character of a written communication. For an idea of different, but influential styles compare advertising copy and newspaper editorials. The former are catchy and readable (although often breaking grammatical rules). The latter are grammatically more correct and wordy, but also less striking. The art of advertising is persuasion; the art of the editorial, comment. In contrast, the role of the feature writer may be information. This style can be different again.

Some technical points of style outlined in the various style manuals (Strunk & White 1971; Baker 1972; Jordan 1982) include the following:

1. *Use the active rather than the passive.* For example, instead of ' . . . those who smoke cigarettes', use ' . . . if you smoke'.

2. *Vary sentence length and construction.* While brevity is important, variety is the spice of reading. Short sentences make an impact; longer sentences are good for developing ideas. Either can be boring if used excessively or exclusively.

3. *Limit paragraphs.* New paragraphs signal a change in thought pattern. In scientific journals these may only come once every five to six sentences. For less literate audiences, and for more striking effect (e.g. when used in advertising) a paragraph may be only one sentence long.

4. *Use transitions.* A transition bridges two sentences or paragraphs. It can take the form of a connecting word ('but', 'also', 'moreover') or a repetition of a word or idea at the end of a sentence.

5. *Learn the grammatical rules, but don't use these religiously.* A glimpse of some of the most persuasive advertising copy shows that the rules don't always apply. Impact in shorter communications can often be increased by starting a sentence with an indefinite article ('And' or 'But'), by using short sentences without verbs, or by ending a sentence with a preposition.

6. *Avoid cliches, slang or 'cute' terms.* Mackay (1986) sums this up in relation to designing marketing promotions to teenagers:

. . . never, never, try to capture the slang or 'code' of the moment. (For example, 'excellent', recently big amongst teenagers, is now strictly primary school, and 'cool' is pre-schoolers' talk. Skateboard language is 'in' but its use by non-boarders appears ridiculous to the cognoscenti.)

Examples of the misuse of this abound, particularly in drug education. 'Rage Without Ruin', 'Smokers Suck' and 'Non-Smokers Rule' are examples of the vernacular which, coming from those outside the peer group, make the target group squirm.

A picture can be worth a thousand lies

(e) Organisation

Order is the soul of written communication. Order is determined, however, by the intended audience and the written form which is intended to be used (e.g. article, ad, news). Information should be organised around a framework and the framework, in turn, based on the intention of the communication.

Organisation therefore is the key. From start to finish, the process should be:

- to titillate (stimulate interest to keep reading)
- to update (provide information—the main aim)
- to consummate (round-off and complete)

Readability formulae

MANY HEALTH PUBLICATIONS, news releases and advertisements have a reading difficulty level above that of many in the target audience. In some cases, it may be useful to actually calculate the difficulty level of the material. Readability formulae provide an objective, systematic, and quantifiable method of analysing the content of written material. A number of formulae exist to measure readability levels. They are developed by studying the relationship of various grammatical (e.g. percentage of prepositional phrases, percentage of abstract nouns, percentage of infrequent words), syntactic (e.g. sentence length, number of phrase units) or morphological (e.g. number of syllables per word) characteristics of the text to readers' scores on comprehension and recall tests using these passages. These formulae objectively and mechanically measure the communication effectiveness of the text as indicated by reader comprehension and recall; they do not involve subjective judgments about aspects such as creativity, imagery or artistic merit.

The Flesch formulae (Flesch 1946, 1947) are the most widely known and used of the readability formulae. They are easy to use, are designed for adult material and are considered more effective and sensitive than other formulae. Flesch derived two readability measures: *reading ease* and *human interest.*

Reading ease is a function of average sentence length (shorter sentences are easier to read) and average word-syllable length (words with fewer syllables are easier to read). Studies cited by Klare (1976) have shown that Flesch's Reading Ease Formula is more reliable to code than more complex formulae.

Human interest is a function of the percentage of 'personal' words in the text and the percentage of 'personal' sentences. Personal words include first-, second- and third-person pronouns except neuter pronouns (e.g. 'it', 'those'), all words that have masculine and feminine genders (e.g. 'John', 'sister', 'mailman') and human group words (e.g. 'people', 'folks'). Personal sentences include spoken sentences and questions, commands, requests and other sentences directly addressed to the reader. Headlines that use personal words (e.g. 'I', 'you', 'we') are particularly effective in attracting attention for both advertising and news items.

Visual imagery

Visual imagery is a powerful medium for both knowledge and attitudes (Rossiter & Percy 1987). Therefore words should be chosen that easily create visual imagery. Concrete words (e.g. 'Fruit 'n veg'; 'tar') are far more powerful for this than abstract words (e.g. 'nutrition', 'carcinogen').

Print type

Print type can influence the 'feel' of a printed document. Selection of typeface, while not altering the content of a message, can significantly affect the way in which this is processed by a reader. Consider the different 'feel' between two different typefaces for the presentation of the following heading:

Health Promotion

Health Promotion

The former is less 'conservative', the latter more 'authoritative'. The latter would be more likely to be seen as coming from a source that could be trusted, the former more from a more flamboyant source.

Moods such as 'relaxed' and 'dreamy' have been associated with curved, light and possibly *sanserif* type; while moods such as 'sad', 'dignified' and 'dramatic' are attached to angular and bold typefaces.

Within typefaces there are a variety of type styles—**bold,** *italics*, CAPITALS, lower case, underlined, outlined—all with different effects and most now available on home desktop computer systems. *Italics* and **bold** for example, are used for headings and emphasis. Lower case is easier to read than UPPER CASE (probably because the upper half of a printed line of type is easier to understand than the bottom half). Hence headlines, although larger and bolder than the body of the text are more effective in lower case. (Check any newspaper for verification of this.)

There is also a link between size of type, line length and space between lines for optimal reading ease. Large type is usually better for older people, but can look childish in some typefaces. Typographical layout can also be used to improve reading ease. Key issues can be summarised in the body of the text for better impact. Regular headings, whether in the middle or to the side of text, have been shown to be effective, particularly with those learning to read who are conceptually less developed and less capable of structuring and organising materials (e.g. lower socio-economic groups, older people, children).

Graphics

There is no doubt that visual images contribute to comprehension and that meanings are easily attached to forms. Some of these are even thought to be so universal that they exist as archetypes in the human psyche (Madigan 1983; Jung 1964). The function of graphics ranges from 'decoration' (e.g. marginally related photographs and drawings), through motivation and organisation (e.g. diagrammatic representation of performance), to information (e.g. physiological diagrams) and entertainment (e.g. cartoons). Realistic drawings are more suited to a serious message, surrealistic drawings

Visuals and indigenous people

As part of the National Campaign Against Drug Abuse a number of graphic posters with culturally relevant anti-drug messages, designed by Aboriginal people, were developed from community-based workshops in Aboriginal communities around Australia. However, although these were popular, the message did not spread throughout communities until they were reproduced onto T-shirts and singlets which were sought after by young Aboriginal people to wear while playing sport.

Making the message culturally relevant

to illustrate an abstract point, and light-hearted cartoons where the message can be inherently entertaining.

Although factors involved in written communications have been studied extensively, those affecting comprehension through pictorial materials have received relatively little attention (Szlichcinski 1980). There is general agreement that illustrations in text serve the following purposes:

- they attract attention to the material and direct attention within the material
- they enhance enjoyment and thus affect emotions and attitudes
- they facilitate learning of text through the improvement of comprehension and retention and by providing additional information

Issues in electronic media

MANY OF THE issues of style discussed for print are also applicable to the electronic media (e.g. brevity, clarity). The differences in skills required for electronic media are obvious, however, from an observation of the limited number of media 'personalities' who can make the transition fluently. Even within electronic media, there are presenters who are effective on radio, but not on television, and vice versa.

Some key issues relevant to the development of electronic media health promotion materials are: the use of a presenter, use of music, voice-overs, voice versus graphics and action tags.

1. Using presenters

All messages are assumed by the target audience to have a source—that is, the individual or organisation perceived to be the author of the message. In some cases, messages also have a presenter—that is, the actual individual or individuals who deliver the message on behalf of the organisation. These presenters may or may not (e.g. as in a voice-over on television) be a prominent part of the message, but they can have considerable influence on message impact, regardless of prominence.

Presenters are of four major types:

1. Unknown, unidentified persons who are selected to deliver the message because of one or more of the following: their professional training, their physical attractiveness and/or their similarity to the target audience.
2. Experts in the area who are chosen to enhance the credibility of the message and hence increase the likelihood of its acceptance.
3. Celebrities who, because of their widespread popularity, are chosen to achieve widespread awareness of the issue (e.g. Elizabeth Taylor's involvement in AIDS); or, because of their popularity with the target audience, are assumed to enhance acceptance of the message and to act as positive role models.
4. Individuals (ordinary or celebrity) who have experienced the health threat and are now suffering, or who have adopted healthy behaviours (i.e. testimonial messages). Ex-drug addicts for example appear to be credible presenters for face-to-face anti-drug and AIDS messages and have been used in safe sex campaigns.

The use of celebrities such as sporting and musical personalities is probably overrated as a means of influencing adolescent behaviour. Recent research suggests that ordinary peer group presenters, and even parents, could be far more effective (Donovan 1991). A further problem with using celebrity presenters is that, in a number of cases, they have been discovered engaging in the behaviours they were employed to speak against. One of the best-known cases of this was the 1950s American actor, James Dean, who was used in a road safety promotion against speeding exhorting teenagers to ' . . . slow down, "cause the life you save could be mine . . . " '. Dean

Celebrities and sporting stars in health promotion

The use of celebrities and sporting stars in health promotion designed to appeal to children has been regarded by some to be an effective method. Serious doubts have now been raised about this by those researching youth attitudes to celebrities (Mackay 1986; Egger 1989). While youth admire the qualities of their heroes, they admire only those qualities with which they agree—not the whole person. If that individual expresses a view contrary to that of the target audience, their view of the desired model may change rather than their view of the desired attitude.

The association of ideals and celebrities is also fraught with other dangers. Sporting stars may have appeal to those heavily involved in those sports, but those interested in sport are unlikely to be smokers in the first place. A typical response of the real target audience to the ad shown below as illustrated in qualitative research is:

'. . . Who gives a ∗∗∗ what Pat Cash thinks anyway.'

was subsequently killed in a head-on collision driving his sports sedan through an intersection in California at over 140 miles per hour.

Some celebrities, because of their public spirited nature, have also become attached to a number of 'public spirited' promotions—from smoking to sexual conduct. This tends to dilute the impact of any message and even water-down the image of the celebrity because of the dismissal or dislike of other characteristics which make up that individual.

In some cases a highly credible source, such as a government department, may be seen as acceptable because of its impartiality and non-profit function. In other cases, a bureaucratic image can work against acceptance of a message. AIDS information is an example of the former; some youth drug campaigns are examples of the latter. Expert authorities can sometimes be used as presenters of health messages. However, it is rare to find health experts with sufficient audience rapport and media presence to give full impact to a message.

Rossiter and Percy (1987) present a checklist for the evaluation and selection of presenters in commercial advertising called 'VisCAP' (Visibility, Credibility, Attraction and Power). Given the provisos spelt out above, this has some application for the use of presenters in health promotion.

2. *The use of Voice-overs*

Electronic media are suited to the use of voice-overs, or recorded voices with or without pictures to carry a message. These can be varied in a number of ways—for example, male/female, deep/high, comic/understanding. The temptation to economise on this aspect of production often leads to the impact of a message being lost because the correct (human) feel has not been added by a professional voice-over.

It is important also to select the voice for the project. A female voice can sound more understanding, whereas a male voice generally represents authority (particularly in areas where male prejudices exist, such as in drinking and smoking).

Similarly, accent and grammar can help to further hone a message to a particular target audience. Accents should never be faked because this can have a counter-productive effect on a group of people who may be openly or sub-consciously sensitive to their speech.

3. *Sound versus graphics*

Health advertising on television may, in some situations, call for the use of graphics rather than voice-over or sound. Graphics are often used where the desired impact is to shock or stun an audience. Rolling graphics on a blank or still screen are most effectively used to arouse fear or empathy—for example, describing the outcome of cancer-causing behaviours:

'YUL BRYNNER DIED, NOT LONG AFTER RECORDING THIS MESSAGE'

(Victorian Anti-Cancer Council, 'Quit Smoking' television advertisement, 1984)

Graphics also can be used to good effect at the end of a television advertisement to reinforce a spoken message—for example:

'QUIT. FOR LIFE!'

(NSW Health Department anti-smoking campaign)

The graphic slogan or conclusion increases the chance of that message being remembered at a later time. Similarly, graphics during a presentation such as an educational video, can be used to reinforce points or summarise conclusions:

  1. Measure Yourself, Don't Weigh Yourself
  2. Reduce Fat Intake
  3. Increase Incidental Exercise
  4. Eat Small Meals Often

(From 'How to Lose Weight', RACGP video 1988)

4. Music

Music is an effective way to get a message across, particularly where:

- rote learning of a slogan or message is an aim
- attention can be drawn by a catchy jingle
- the target audience consists of youth
- picture stories in visual media call for supplementation

Jingles accompanying short ad promotions need to be framed in the tone of the target audience. They need also to be short, intensive and have a chorus line that contains the main message component and which stands out from the jingle. This is often accompanied by a spoken voice-over repeat of a slogan or message on the visual media (TV, video, film) with graphic support (i.e. the words in print).

The technical requirements of jingles makes these a highly specialised form of communication. An advertiser or health promotion practitioner can approach a professional jingle writer with a basic idea, or even lyrics. The writer is then given the task of setting the words to music. Jingles are a particularly useful form of promotion where a campaign approach is called for. Campaign themes, action themes and catchy messages can be summed up in jingle form.

5. Action tags

These call for potential follow-up action on the part of the target audience. An action tag (phone number to ring, place to visit, address to write to), should be part of every press release, news item, booklet or advertisement. Action tags not only encourage follow-up action, but help the program designer evaluate the effectiveness of a promotion. In some cases (i.e. 'Quit Smoking' advertisements), action tags can be used to elicit commitment from the message receiver. A message for the audience to register their name as part of a quit program has the effect, however illusory, that the responder is being 'watched'. Messages with action tags should be repeated regularly within an exposure period so they become entrenched in the mind of the receiver, who can then take up the option to act at some later time.

The Method

THE THREE MAIN methods of media use we have chosen to focus on are advertising, publicity and 'edutainment'. Other less prominent methods are considered in Chapter 11. Of the three main methods, advertising is clearly the most visible in commercial marketing. This is because it is the most used, and unlike publicity and entertainment, is clearly identified as commercial marketing. However, much of what we see and hear in the news and current affairs, and in feature articles in the print media, are in fact press releases from various organisations. Governments, in particular, are prolific providers of material. Similarly, there is increasing product placement in television programs and, via sponsorship of sporting and other events, in photographs and video news of such events.

Advertising is probably the most visible of these methods in health promotion, particularly in Australia. Publicity is also widely used, but edutainment rarely forms part of a comprehensive communication campaign. Advertising is also generally the most-used method, at least by well-funded campaigns, because it is the only way of ensuring exposure of the intended message to the intended target audience in a specific time frame.

As pointed out earlier (see Chapter 4), 'advocacy' is often included as an additional method in some health promotion literature. However, we regard advocacy as a role of the media that can be achieved through any of the above methods. It is '. . . the strategic use of mass media for advancing a social or public policy initiative' (Wallack 1990). Advocacy uses any or all of these media methods to focus attention on the way a problem is understood as a health issue, rather than on changing individual risk behaviour. It is directed at structural, rather than individual change and attempts to move from the ' "individual-simple" to the "social/political-complex" part of the problem definition continuum'. (Wallack 1990). Usually, because of the insufficiency of funds available, advocacy involves publicity rather than advertising or edutainment. However, advocacy can come through edutainment, or indeed be an objective or outcome of successfully targeted health promotion advertising.

Advertising, publicity and edutainment are considered in detail over the next three chapters.

9

Delivering the message through advertising

To be most effective, an ad must generate both 'light' (cognition) and 'heat' (emotion). (Rossiter, Percy & Donovan 1984)

ADVERTISING IS THE art of communicating to sell products and/or services. Contrary to popular opinion, it is not new and has existed in one form or another for centuries. Indeed, a quote from a 1759 issue of the *Idler* is reported to have read: 'The trade of advertising is now so near to perfection that it is not easy to propose any improvement' (Bevins 1987).

Advertising, in the commercial sense, has two main aims:

1. to increase overall consumption of a product or service, and/or
2. to increase the competitive share of existing sales for a product or service

In general it matters little to the advertiser which of these goals is met; the desired outcome—increased profits—is the same.

From a health point of view, increases in consumption of certain products (e.g. high-fat foods), can have negative consequences. Even normal consumption of some products (e.g. cigarettes) is regarded as unhealthy. Cigarette promoters have been quick to point out that advertising of their product is aimed at increasing market share rather than increasing the total market, despite the fact that a major rationale of advertising as expressed by the Advertising Association of Australia (AAA), is to assist economic growth by increasing consumption.

Advertising can therefore be both a boon and a bane to health promotion. On the one hand it has facilitated the development of sophisticated techniques of persuasion which, it has been presumed, could also be used to *decrease* consumption of unhealthy products and *increase* the adoption of healthy behaviours. On the other hand, it has been used (with only limited restraints) over long periods to increase consumption and behaviours which are contrary to public health. The latter use has been argued frequently in the literature in relation to alcohol (Neuendorf 1987), cigarettes (Tye, Warner & Glantz 1988) and unhealthy food consumption (Australian Consumers' Association 1982).

Agitation on the part of health authorities has led to the development of voluntary advertising codes for cigarette and alcohol advertising and the banning of cigarette advertising from electronic media in 1975. Codes have offered an aid to health workers, although it is acknowledged that these have had only limited success (Drew 1982).

The role of advertising in the (marketing) communications mix

ALTHOUGH WE HAVE stated that the aim of commercial advertising is to influence consumption, this is not meant to imply that advertising alone can, or does, bring about behaviour change. As our discussion of the four Ps in Chapter 3 noted, all elements of the marketing mix (*product, price, place* and *promotion*) must act together to effectively influence behaviour. Furthermore, advertising is generally only one element of an integrated marketing communications mix, the other elements being public relations and publicity, personal selling, and sales promotions. Each of these has their own, but complementary, objectives in a specific campaign.

For example, to launch a new product, extensive advertising may be carried out to create awareness and a tentative positive attitude toward the product; press releases may be issued about the product's technological characteristics, its social benefits or its ecological soundness; special sales representatives may be on hand in-store to describe and operate the product; and entry to a sweepstake plus a substantial discount may be offered to the first 100 purchasers. That is, in most commercial campaigns, advertising having a defined but limited set of objectives, is only one element of an integrated campaign.

In many early (and even some recent) health promotion campaigns, advertising has been the only, or primary component, with no, or only lip-service, paid to other elements of the social marketing mix. Needless to say, many of these campaigns were failures, leading to unwarranted criticism of the usefulness of advertising per se.

The role of advertising in health promotion campaigns

IN LINE WITH Rossiter and Percy's (1987) objectives for commercial advertising, the objectives for health promotion advertising can be listed as follows:

1. Creating, maintaining or increasing awareness of an issue, product, service or event.
2. Creating, maintaining or increasing positive attitudes towards an issue, product, service or event.

3. Creating, maintaining or increasing explicit or implicit intentions to behave in the recommended manner (including intermediate behaviours).
4. Neutralising misperceptions and negatives and justifying costs and other factors that inhibit adoption of the recommended behaviour.

In most cases, the major roles of advertising are firstly, to create awareness of the issue and secondly, to create a tentative positive attitude toward the issue that predisposes the individual to other components of the campaign and to positive social pressures. The extent to which advertising can directly influence behaviour in the health field depends on the nature of the behaviour and the extent of prior public education. For example, non threatening one-off behaviours such as cholesterol testing, and even one-off behaviours with quite threatening consequences such as HIV testing, can be influenced directly by advertising campaigns (in conjunction with easily accessible test sites). However, addictive and more complex behaviours requiring substantial lifestyle changes can rarely be influenced directly by advertising. Advertising's role in these latter instances is to maintain awareness of the issue, to provide directions to sources of assistance, and to generate positive attitudes towards the desired behaviour change.

Effective public health advertising

DONOVAN (1991) HAS developed a series of guidelines for effective public health advertising which he divides into *general media guidelines* and *message guidelines*. These are discussed below.

General media guidelines

Advertising should be preceded and accompanied by authoritative publicity

It is essential that health messages be credible. Hence, it is important, particularly in 'new' areas of health that public health advertising be preceded by extensive publicity. For example, the 1953 Sloan-Kettering Report that linked cancer in rats to tar from cigarette smoke, and the 1964 United States Surgeon General's report that linked smoking to lung cancer not only resulted in an immediate reduction of smoking, but also provided major support for subsequent quit smoking programs. Similarly, AIDS education programs in the United States received a substantial boost following release of the Surgeon General's Report on AIDS in 1986.

Use intrusive media (for most target groups)

For most health issues, it is unlikely that the vast majority of those practising an unhealthy behaviour will be actively seeking information contrary to that behaviour. Indeed, it could be presumed that many would actively avoid information that creates anxiety about their unhealthy behaviour.

What is an advertising agency?

Advertising agencies function as a link between advertisers and the media. Their original function was to sell advertising space in magazines and newspapers, for which the publishers paid the agencies a commission.

$$\boxed{\text{ADVERTISER}} \leftarrow \boxed{\text{AD AGENCY}} \rightarrow \boxed{\text{MEDIA}}$$

Agencies still derive the major part of their income from such commissions, but they now also have other roles including:

1. Advising on advertising strategy.
2. Developing and producing advertising.
3. Determining a media schedule.
4. Placing the advertising in the media.

Agencies who perform all of these roles are called 'full-service' agencies. Some large agencies now prefer to focus on the strategic and creative side of advertising and leave the media scheduling and placement function to specialist media buying agencies. Other smaller agencies (often called 'boutique' agencies) offer only a creative service.

Although many full-service agencies prefer large clients, many try to allot time to social causes. Some agencies even see health organisation accounts as prestigious and useful background when tendering competitively for large budget campaigns such as the 'Drug Offensive'.

Television, radio and outdoor media are intrusive. Print advertising and brochures are not. For this reason, print is more appropriate for reaching members of the target audience who are already motivated to carry out a particular behaviour (e.g. quit smoking, moderate drinking, seek more information about AIDS).

Television, because of its intrusiveness, is clearly the primary medium for public health campaigns targeting substantial proportions of the population. Television provides rapid penetration of (most) target audience(s) and can be both educational and motivational. Television also allows the simplification of complex processes by animated and/or graphic illustration of the negative health effects of unhealthy practices. Furthermore, television allows the modelling of correct behaviours.

Scheduling: short intensive periodic campaigns appear most effective

In general, the most effective public health advertising campaigns appear to be those which are short but intensive and periodic. Infrequent exposures over a long period can achieve a high reach, but because of their infrequency, can be ineffective. On the other hand, campaigns that are sustained at very high levels for too long can also be ineffective because the audience becomes desensitised. Given that much health advertising needs to be dramatic, desensitisation may be a greater problem than it is with commercial campaigns. To retain the impact, short bursts of advertising rather than a

Using an advertising agency—the ad brief

Selling health is not like selling soap powder. The former generally requires promoting complex changes in behaviour, for little immediate reward, with no tangible product. Hence, while it's often necessary in a health promotion campaign to work with creative advertising personnel, it should not be taken for granted that these people know about health promotion. It's our experience that advertising experts let loose on a health promotion campaign need a good deal of experience before understanding the subtleties of the art. This is aided by the use of tight, accurate and easily understood creative briefs. The brief should detail answers to the questions posed by the planning process detailed in Chapter 2—that is:

1. The overall objectives for the advertising.
2. Details of the target audience(s) (including demographics, media habits, current behaviours, beliefs and attitudes towards the issue in question).
3. The behavioural objectives (if any, and including intermediate behaviours).
4. The communication objectives (i.e. the target beliefs and attitudes).
5. The message strategy necessary to achieve the communication objectives.
6. Media vehicle recommendations (if any).
7. The production and media budgets.

An ad brief should be short and succinct, and is best accompanied by a verbal presentation to ad agency personnel.

continuous schedule, are often called for, and these can be provided by a pool of ads which promote variations on a theme.

Periodic short bursts of advertising are particularly applicable to campaigns with specific behavioural objectives (e.g. quitting smoking, alcohol moderation, fat reduction and exercise adoption) that target Prochaska's 'ready for action' segment. In these cases, and particularly with respect to smoking, it appears that most behaviour modification appears early in the advertising campaign. Hence, to conserve funds, it is recommended that the duration of such campaigns be limited to about four weeks. Where it is necessary to sustain promotions to maintain risk-reducing behaviour (e.g. AIDS prevention), a large source of funds and a large pool of ads would be necessary to prevent desensitisation.

Media infiltration: the principle of social proof

'Social proof' is a concept developed to explain the observation that individuals use the actions of others, including those portrayed in the media, to decide appropriate behaviours and attitudes. Alcohol and cigarette company sponsorship of sporting and cultural events are clear messages (to children and adolescents in particular), that smoking and drinking are 'endorsed' by society. Furthermore, marketers pay large amounts of money to have their brands prominently displayed in movies and TV programs.

Advertising campaigns can support social norms and they appear to be most effective when supported by publicity, health sponsorships and other, non-advertising media exposure.

Realistic goals should be set

Unrealistic goals can reduce the effectiveness of a campaign attempting to influence complex health-related behaviours. Hence feasible, middle-range goals need to be established and outcomes clearly identified for evaluation. For advertising campaign components, these relate to relevance for the target audience, awareness and under-standing of the issue, attitudes towards the issue and other elements of the intervention. Only when the ad calls for a specific behaviour to which there are no major barriers, should behavioural measures be part of the evaluation of the advertising.

Message guidelines

The message should be single minded with respect to message content and target audience

Because of the complexity of health messages and inexperience of health professionals as communicators, there is often a tendency to overload health messages with infor-mation. While this may not be a disadvantage for a feature article in a magazine targeted at an educated audience, it is a distinct disadvantage in advertising where short, impactful messages are required. Hence, single mindedness is imperative. In short, the aim should be to select one target audience and one major message (or related set of messages) for that target audience, for each advertisement.

Credibility is essential

To minimise the rejection of a message (which may make the receiver uncomfortable), it is essential that health education advertising be believable. Non-credible advertis-ing—even if it is true (but not *credible* to the receiver)—is likely to be counter-pro-ductive since it may lessen the audience assessment that ' . . . this could happen to me'. For this reason it is important not to exaggerate the effects of a behaviour and the likelihood of occurrence of adverse effects resulting from that behaviour. Drink-driving advertising suggesting death and destruction as a result of offending behaviour is unlikely to have a significant effect because it is generally perceived that 'this only happens to bad drivers—it wouldn't happen to me'.

Careful strategy and pretesting research are necessary to ensure that the message claims stay within the target audience's 'latitude of acceptance'. Pretesting is particularly important where celebrities are used and for presentations which depict the target audience in 'typical' situations. In these supposedly typical situations, the authenticity of the actors, the language style and the situation itself are critical for establishing empathy with the target audience.

The message should be personalised

Personalisation of a message is illustrated by a cartoon in a United States' newspaper in 1989 which showed two people looking out a window at an aeroplane towing a message which read: 'Maury Blivet in Apt 23A, the Surgeon General has determined

'Here's to the iron willed Wollongong drinker'

Topic: Drink driving.

Sponsoring organisation: Australian Medical Association.

Background: Motor vehicle injury in young drink-drivers was a major concern in the industrial city of Wollongong in 1984. Focus group research suggested a positive approach for acceptance in a population of lower-education-level young men with a high rate of unemployment.

Objectives:
1. To change attitudes to drinking and driving in young men through developing a responsible image of a 'good drinker'.
2. To improve the public image of the AMA as a concerned, public-spirited professional association.

Media: TV; radio (music jingle); booklet; professional (doctor) materials; T-shirts.

Market: Unemployed, lower-education level, male drinkers aged 18–25 who identify themselves as from Wollongong.

Message: Good drinkers don't drink and drive.

Method: Advertising.

Measures: Reduction of vehicle injuries of 40% in the media period. Change of attitudes to drinking and driving by young drivers.

Source: Reznick et al. (1984).

that smoking is hazardous to your health specifically.' The most personal health information (and that which is regarded as generally most effective) comes from an individual's physician. Hence, the closer a media message can be made to the personal 'doctor–patient' type interaction, the more impact that message is likely to have.

There are standard techniques to personalise a message in print advertising (e.g. a self-assessment questionnaire). For other media, other means may need to be used. Arousal of relevant anxiety may be useful for television, as is the use of testimonials by individuals with whom the viewer can identify. Testimonials using gay men for example, have been widely used to combat the first wave of the AIDS epidemic; teenage accident victims can have appeal to other teenagers where doctors or adults would be expected to have little impact.

Fear is fine—sometimes!

The use of fear in health communications has had a varied history. Early studies in drug education suggested that fear arousal may be counter-productive in attempting to discourage drug abuse. Yet while this may be true in some groups, mild fear-provoking messages presented in a lively and entertaining way have been shown to be effective in a variety of situations (Sutton 1982).

In general, negative emotions (anxiety, fear and guilt) are major motivators for change in health-related behaviour. These can often be tapped to encourage more rapid behaviour change—provided fear is handled in a delicate and sensitive fashion! According to Job (1988), there are a number of guidelines for making fear effective. These are:

1. The onset of fear should occur before the desired behaviour is offered.
2. The event upon which the fear is based should appear to be likely.
3. A specific desired behaviour should be offered as part of the campaign.
4. The level of fear elicited should only be such that the desired behaviour offered is sufficient to substantially reduce the fear.
5. Fear offset should occur as a reinforcer for the desired behaviour, confirming its effectiveness.

In using fear in a communication it is important to distinguish between arousing anxiety and arousing horror or revulsion. It has long been known, for example, (Higbee 1969) that fear can be either inhibitory or anticipatory. Inhibitory fear refers to fear aroused by horror, and this generally results in efforts to reduce the anxiety (e.g. by not looking at the ad, by denial). Anticipatory fear, on the other hand, is aroused by concern about the likelihood of experiencing a threat, and this results in more realistic actions being taken to deal with the *threat* itself rather than avoiding the *anxiety*.

Some health campaigns (e.g. early road trauma prevention and anti-smoking campaigns) focused too much on the revulsion and horror, and not enough on personal anxiety arousal resulting from the perception that 'this could happen to me'. Messages such as these, that concentrate too much on fear, risk attention being distracted from the message in the same way that commercial marketers who focus on sex and humour in their advertising run the risk of this being the prime attention grabber, and not their message.

The use of fear in health advertising

The use of fear as a health promotion tactic has been a controversial issue, to the extent that it was largely discarded in the 1970s. Ads such as the award-winning 'Lung is like a sponge' commercial and the one shown here challenged this. Fear is now regarded as useful under certain conditions, provided a solution to fear reduction is easily available and that the fear is based on a personal likelihood of an event happening, rather than simply on exposure to an horrific scene.

Offer a solution

Health promotion advertising, and particularly that which provokes anxiety, should offer the means to obtaining a solution. This can be either indirect, as in fear-provoking messages, or more direct, as offered through an action tag. It is important also to ensure that not only are the means of averting a threat or obtaining promised benefits as simple as possible, but also that the individual is capable of implementing the proposed solution. Much has been written about the latter issue (self efficacy) as being of key importance in much health-related behaviour.

Emphasise the ME in MESsage

Although times change, individuals in general are motivated primarily to behave out of self interest and not for the benefit of others. Appeals to community spirit and collective moralism therefore, while effective in some areas of government policy, should not always be expected to have the desired impact on personal health behaviour. Hence messages directed at drink-drivers to be 'responsible citizens' are far less effective than drink-driving campaigns that emphasise not only the severity of the penalty if caught, but the high probability of the individual being caught. Visibility of police on the roads, or if this is not possible, *perceived* visibility (e.g. via ads emphasising the extent of random breath testing), may be expected to contribute to changes in behaviour much more than appeals to social conscience.

Yet while self interest is a powerful motivator, there are some qualifying considerations. Consumer research suggests that while men clearly respond best to self-interest-only appeals, women do respond to appeals that include both self interest and concern for others (Myers-Levy 1988). Hence it may be appropriate to target women with a dual-appeal approach. Also, trends in self interest may vary over time. Although Thomas Wolfe succinctly defined the 1970s' and 1980s' philosophy in western society as that of a 'Me Generation', interests in pollution, the environment and global issues in the 1990s indicates a change in thinking to a 'We Generation' which may be essential for global survival.

Be dramatic!

Drama in health advertising tends to (a) stimulate public comment and therefore expand the natural reach of a campaign; and (b) have a direct affect in socially influencing behaviours through word-of-mouth contact. Hence advertising should be designed to be dramatic and stimulate social discussion of the advertising message. Care should be taken, however, not to be dramatic just for the sake of it. Rather, ad executions must be dramatic in the way that they communicate the intended message. Ads will be less effective if the drama simply generates discussion of the execution.

Be controversial (if appropriate)

Health promotion is often by nature controversial. This can be used to advantage in certain situations to create controversy that may positively affect a campaign in the long term.

As well as open controversy, research has shown the effects of counter-argument in establishing long-term behaviour change (Roberts & Maccoby 1985). This appears to be most successful where an audience is resistant and initially opposed to an idea, or is well educated and likely to be exposed to opposition messages. If this approach is used, however, it is important to expose the weaknesses in the opposition argument and provide the receiver of the message with information with which to combat opposing views.

Use modelling

Modelling is the basis of much of children's learning and is a powerful technique for encouraging the adoption of behaviours. Commercial marketers use modelling to show people how to order, use or consume products, and, in the case of cigarettes and alcohol, how to share these around in a social situation. There are a number of opportunities for modelling in health promotion campaigns (e.g. how to say 'no', 'quit tips', tips to reduce alcohol consumption, breast cancer self-examination techniques). Bevins (1987) has described a dramatic case of the effectiveness of modelling the 'Quit' line in his quit smoking advertisements. Calls to a 'Quit' line, that had been previously advertised as an action tag only, jumped from approximately 350 per week to 12 000 per week after the broadcast of footage showing a smoker watching the previously aired quit smoking advertisement on his television, and then reaching for the phone and dialling the 'Quit' line.

Provide supporting reasons

Manufacturers of high-prestige motor cars need to provide supporting reasons for the purchase of their product as there may be personal resistance to buying on a purely social-image basis. Similarly, health marketers need to provide target audiences with a number of reasons to support adoption of the desired behaviour change. This is particularly relevant where the targeted individual will be subjected to peer pressure to maintain an undesirable health practice. With young audiences, for example, where health effects are not an acceptable peer defence for alcohol moderation or avoiding drugs, other supporting reasons are needed. These may take the form of more immediate health effects (e.g. fitness), or social disapproval consequences of the particular behaviour (e.g. bad breath for young smokers). Similarly, for exercise, the positive motivations of social approval and the need for achievement can be used to support health reasons for regular exercise.

Be 'cool'

Attitude change in high-involvement decision making is more effective when explicit conclusions are not made in the message content, but are left to be drawn by the individual audience members. Where a conclusion is drawn in an ad, this is called a 'hot' message by communication researchers; where the conclusion is not explicitly drawn this is called a 'cool' message.

Health advertising must be seen by the target audience as informative and entertaining, but not dictatorial. This is particularly important for ads aimed at young children and teenagers, and at widespread community behaviours such as smoking and alcohol.

Show highly visible effects

The clear demonstration of harmful effects is likely to generate a 'happening to me' self-assessment. Similarly, showing non-hospitalised persons whose everyday activities are severely impeded by a disability related to the issue in question (e.g. a person with a tracheostomy resulting from throat cancer caused by smoking) appears to be more effective than showing bedridden inactive victims.

Young persons in particular, probably due to a greater concern than older persons for body-image and body-wholeness, appear particularly susceptible to potential disabling effects, rather than to threats of death at some long-term future date.

Controversial media: a way of increasing the health promotion dollar

1. The introduction of the 'Grim Reaper' in the early 1980s as a warning against AIDS created a public outcry because of its fear tactics. The campaign had no long-term health promotion follow-up, which perhaps limited its long-term effectiveness. However, as a result of the controversy created (and of course, the topic), the 'Grim Reaper' had a much greater impact than a less controversial approach. (see picture on page 117).

2. A quit smoking campaign in the late 1980s developed for the NSW Health Department showed a fish hook coming from the filter of a cigarette and embedding itself in the lip of a young female smoker. The TV image was a powerful demonstration of the addictiveness of smoking. Initially, the ad was banned, then allowed to run after protest, but only after the penetration of the hook into the lip was covered in early evening viewing. The censored version made children much more aware of the real ad, and it thus had a greater impact.

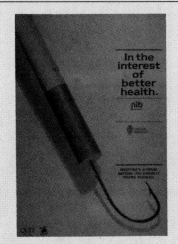

Use high-imagery symbols and words

Concrete stimuli are far more effective in generating visual imagery than are abstract stimuli, and the generation of visual imagery enhances both the credibility and the retention of the message. One particularly effective TV advertisement made for the New South Wales Department of Health likens the human lung to a sponge 'that soaks up tar'. The sponge is shown inside a smoking mannequin, expanding and contracting like a lung. At the end of the advertisement the sponge is wrung out into a beaker to show the amount of 'cancer-producing tar' absorbed by the average smoker over a period of time. This advertisement appears to encourage smokers to assess directly the impact of smoking on their lungs.

Use simple mnemonics

Where the target behaviours result in clearly defined ill-health effects in specific organs of the body, mnemonic techniques can be used to get the information across. Such mnemonics can serve not only as memory aids, but can also lead to more effective self assessment on the part of the individual.

For example, in an alcohol-moderation campaign in Western Australia, a voice-over explains alcohol's effects on various organs of the body, while a hand is seen placing needles into the corresponding anatomical locations of a doll. Similar mnemonic campaigns have been used in the United Kingdom to show the effects of heroin on

various parts of the body. Pretesting showed presentations involving these sorts of mnemonic techniques to be more effective than various alternative presentations of the same health message.

Use presenters carefully

Credibility is a major requirement for all high-involvement messages and has been found to enhance the impact of fear appeals. High source credibility makes it more difficult for the target audience to reject the validity of the message. This is particularly important for anxiety-arousing health messages.

For low- or medium-risk young persons, the use of parents as presenters should be considered. While celebrities (and expert presenters) may enhance prescriptive norms, the use of ordinary members of the target group may be used to give the impression that the desired behaviour is more widespread than previously thought, and particularly in testimonials to increase the subjective probability of the outcome (i.e. enhance personal assessment of risk). Expert presenters and testimonials are also useful for enhancing the credibility of messages.

Lifestyle executions (a derivative of the testimonial approach) are becoming more popular both in Australia and overseas. Showing appropriate lifestyle models and consumption situations in advertisements targeted to specific lifestyle groups enhances attention to, and acceptance of, the message, by arousing empathy with the target audience.

Ensure congruent portrayal of prescriptive and popular norms

Social advertising executions can be weakened if the execution includes a conflict between prescriptive norms (i.e. socially desired behaviours) and popular norms (i.e. behaviours typically performed). For example, anti-litter ads may actually promote littering because they suggest that littering behaviour is widespread. Hence those influenced by popular, rather than prescriptive, norms may be unaffected by such advertisements or may even have their littering behaviour reinforced. In Western Australia, an early anti-smoking advertisement aimed at adults announced that '40 000 children smoke in Western Australia'. While such an advertisement may indeed arouse parents, children might be influenced to the contrary on the basis of 'social proof' (see Chapter 2).

Summary

THE INDIVIDUAL DETERMINANTS of power of execution do not operate independently. They are highly interrelated. Executional elements that generate a self assessment are generally the same sorts of elements that enhance credibility. Presentations that are more credible and personal are generally those that arouse strong relevant emotions. Those showing concrete effects tend to be more credible and create a stronger self assessment. 'Getting it right' in one area enhances the likelihood of getting it right in other areas.

In summary, the crucial techniques for public health advertising appear to be the following:

1. Be credible, don't exaggerate claims.
2. Arouse a strong, relevant emotional response, whether this is positive or negative.
3. For fear appeals, show relevant, disabling harmful effects in otherwise healthy individuals rather than bedridden patients, and ensure that anxiety results from a relevant self assessment rather than from the executional elements per se.
4. Be sufficiently dramatic to generate word-of-mouth about the message (i.e. not just about the way in which it was presented).
5. Use simple, concrete words and visual demonstrations of effects—both positive and negative.
6. Show a means of attaining the desired behaviour and a source of assistance.
7. Use modelling to encourage the trial and adoption of behavioural objectives.
8. Use mnemonics for information objectives.
9. Where relevant, ensure that prescriptive norms and popular norms are congruent.

Co-operation advertising

MOST HEALTH AGENCIES, especially small local agencies, will have funds only for a small amount of advertising. One way to extend the advertising budget is to seek co-operation with a commercial health organisation or an organisation that promotes its products with a valid health claim: for example, health clubs, health insurance companies, fruit and vegetable co-operatives, and 'healthy' food marketers. In many cases, both in Australia and overseas, it has been the commercial organisations that have approached the health organisations for assistance.

For example, in the United States in 1984, the Kellogg company approached the National Cancer Institute (NCI) to seek implicit endorsement for its All-Bran cereal in return for including NCI's dietary guidelines in advertising, and its Cancer Information Service toll-free number and dietary guidelines on the pack. Kellogg's campaign had a positive effect on people's awareness of fibre as a beneficial diet component (Freimuth, Hammond & Stein 1988). In Australia, MBF Health Insurance works closely with health authorities in advertising mammogram screening, NIB Health Funds are a major sponsor of the 'GutBusters' program (see Chapter 12), and fresh produce marketers have supported health authority 'fruit 'n veg' campaigns.

Sponsorship

RECENT YEARS HAVE seen the establishment of a number of health promotion foundations in Australia. Although each state's foundations differ somewhat in their specific objectives and functions, most (at least to some extent) serve as a source of funds for health organisations to sponsor sport, racing and arts events that may have benefited previously from tobacco company sponsorship.

Many such sponsorships are limited to matters such as signage at the event, ticket and program advertisements, and perhaps announcements over the public address system, and reach only those at the event. However, others can receive extensive publicity in the media, particularly if celebrities are associated with the promotion, or if a newsworthy item is created for the event. Some sponsorships may reach only those at the event, but because there is a series of events involving repeat attenders (i.e. a sporting season promotion), the sponsorship provides an opportunity for message reinforcement.

As for commercial perimeter advertising, where mass media coverage is obtained for a health message sponsorship, this provides an opportunity to maintain the awareness of the health message or slogan, as well as reinforce a perception of the social norm or social acceptance of the message.

Concluding comment

ALTHOUGH ADVERTISING CAN be expensive, it is generally a necessary component of most campaigns that attempt to reach large numbers of people in a limited time frame and with a high level of control over information input. Advertising serves the very useful purpose of creating rapid awareness of an issue; legitimising the issue as one of community concern (i.e. agenda setting); creating a positive context within which to introduce specific interventions; directing people to sources of assistance and information and to community action events. Given appropriate circumstances, it may also contribute significantly to the desired behaviour, whether this be an individual risk behaviour change or participation in a community action event.

10

Delivering the message through publicity

*P*UBLICITY, IN CONTRAST to advertising, generally revolves around 'news'. News can be either an event or promotion designed to stimulate involvement in health activities, or news of interest about aspects of health, including new scientific findings and socio-political influences.

News through publicity can be used to educate (or inform) about a point of view, or to motivate (or persuade) towards doing a certain action. Advocacy is a third role of publicity, and indeed it is through publicity that advocacy is generally achieved. One of the best examples of media advocacy in health promotion is the recent (i.e. since the 1980s) approach by many media to news relating to cigarette smoking and health. Not only are the dangers of smoking now presented in the mass media much more widely and accurately than in the past, but there is also more open discussion about effects about which there is less scientific proof, such as passive smoking, smoking and facial wrinkles or smoking and sexual attraction. The media have also facilitated discussion about changing a system which allows open promotion of tobacco products.

Three factors have made advocacy for reduced smoking more possible:

1. the ban on tobacco advertising in many media, thus releasing them from commercial pressures
2. increased and more sophisticated scientific support against smoking
3. a long-term background of quit smoking health promotions which have 'sensitised' the public to acceptance of this message

This has no doubt resulted in a form of 'differential association' (Strickland 1978; Lewis et al. 1989), a term used to describe changes in social norms which somehow occur spontaneously and change the way in which an issue is perceived in the community. This centres on the influence of family, friends, the media and health experts (Pelto 1981; Sims 1987).

Advocacy involves using skills to 'create' news and encourage the media to report this in a way that can educate and/or motivate to improve health or facilitate structural and social change that is more conducive to better health. The process of advocacy is currently the source of much discussion and debate with some recent publications dealing with it in detail (see Chapman et al. 1993).

Advocacy involves some of the basic procedures for publicity, such as:

* issuing media releases
* staging press conferences
* writing for publication
* staging publicity events

Advocacy actions do extend further than this, however, and can also involve other media methods such as advertising and edutainment, as discussed in Chapter 5.

Public relations and publicity

THE TWO TERMS, 'public relations' and 'publicity', are often confused. For our purposes we regard publicity as just one tool, albeit a major one, of public relations. Overall, public relations refers to the creation and maintenance of goodwill towards the company and its products by its various 'publics'. Unlike advertising, which is targeted primarily towards the organisation's consumers (or primary target audience), public relations is concerned with all of the organisation's publics. For commercial organisations these may include its employees, shareholders, suppliers, distributors, consumer lobby groups, trade and general media journalists, and its consumers. The lesson for health promotion professionals is to recognise that the success of many campaigns, whether mass media or community based, depends on establishing good-will with, and the co-operation of, a number of organisations or groups (known as 'stakeholders'), as well as the primary target group (see Egger, Donovan & Spark 1990).

Advocating for a cleaner Australia

Although the now annual 'Clean Up Australia Day' was started in 1987 as an individual initiative by Sydney yachtsman Ian Kiernan, it has grown to involve 400 000 participants throughout Australia in 5 142 sites in 1992. This has come about largely through the effective use of media publicity and public relations including, in recent years, community service advertising and widespread advocacy throughout all levels of the media.

Source: McKay & Gasal 1992.

An example from the commercial field is that of sugar. Faced with declining sugar consumption in Australia in the late 1970s and early 1980s, the Colonial Sugar Refining company (CSR) mounted a successful campaign to change consumer attitudes toward

---

What is a public relations (PR) organisation?

Public relations organisations specialise in creating favourable public images for organisations, products or events. Although having a different role from advertising, PR work can involve advertising, and PR organisations often work in conjunction with (although sometimes also see themselves in competition with) advertising agencies. In general, the PR organisation will be concerned with events, publicity, news and happenings that are less controllable with respect to information output than paid advertisements.

In health promotion campaigns, a PR company is often used to generate ongoing publicity, execute a media 'launch' and organise media events, making the issue newsworthy. An advertising agency is used simply to generate and place advertisements.

---

sugar consumption. This campaign involved not only extensive television advertising to consumers, (based on the theme of sugar being 'a natural part of life'), but also extensive public relations efforts toward federal and state government legislators, medical and dental practitioners, pharmacists, nutritionists, food industry associations, the media and sugar industry employees (Ivest 1988). The turnaround in attitudes to, and consumption of, sugar as a result of the campaign is an indication of the power of an effectively delivered message and a highly skilled public relations campaign in influencing behaviours which are health related.

Public relations (PR) involves a number of activities, only some of which are media related. Public relations tools include employee magazines, educational materials, annual reports, research funding and charitable donations, as well as press releases, press conferences, staging of special events to attract media coverage, and other media activities. We will refer to these media activities as 'publicity'.

Publicity is distinguished from advertising because while professional public relations persons may be paid to develop these messages or to assist in their placement, there is no payment to the media for such placement, nor is there control over the timing or position of the message in the media vehicle.

There is also the problem of control over message content. Messages are either supplied to the media in the form of press releases, or are generated by the media from interviews with the message source, coverage of publicity events, or extracted from materials supplied by the source or from the journalist's own investigations. In all of these cases, it is the media who decide what will or will not actually appear. In only a few cases such as 'live' broadcast interviews, talkback radio and verbatim reports in print media, is the message presented without editing by the media.

One of the major tools of publicity is the staging of attention-getting events. Publicity, or news coverage derived from staged events, differs from most other PR activities in that it involves some action (rather than just a message), is far less formal and generally involves a number of direct participants (rather than just a media audience). Such events may also serve a fund-raising function (e.g. a walkathon).

Planning a media publicity campaign
What is news?

News is an 'event' or 'statement' which is interesting, important, exciting or informative to anyone who may be affected by it. 'Hard news' is the term given to news of world events or local events of a major nature. 'Soft news' is generally non-emotive events of interest to a limited audience. Most health promotion news is 'soft news' which has to compete with 'hard news' for media space.

The art of communicating health through media publicity is in making 'soft news' more appealing, by making it:

- interesting
- relevant
- exciting
- informative
- amusing
- personally or financially profitable

News does not always just 'happen'. It is often created. Once it is created, it then has to be told to someone in the media in a fashion that will make it interesting and exciting enough to be able to successfully compete with a lot of other individuals and groups (many of them highly organised) trying to do the same thing. To compete, the health promotion practitioner has to have a plan:

- Decide what you want to say—keep it to a couple of simple clear points.
- Decide who you are trying to say it to. Is it news to them?
- Decide where and when you want to say it, so that it will most effectively reach your target audience.
- Decide why you want to say it.

One of the most important first steps is in knowing who, when and how to contact the media.

Who to contact in the media

Large newspaper—chief of staff

Local newspaper—editor

TV or radio newsroom—news editor

Special TV or radio program—producer or researcher

If a good relationship has been developed with a particular journalist, that person may be the only contact needed. It is very important to check the spelling of his or her name. You can make friends with journalists in the following ways:

- Don't repeat second-hand information. Check the source and provide the source to the journalist.
- Give few (but accurate) stories, rather than many paper chases. This way you'll maintain credibility with the journalist.
- If you give wrong information unwittingly, correct yourself as soon as possible.
- Be prepared to be contacted at all times of the day and night.
- Seek out and cultivate journalists who will be useful to you. Even the most junior reporters, if they do their job well, get promoted. Help them to do it well.
- Take the trouble to ring and thank a reporter after a good story.
- Don't be offended if a friendly reporter tells you your story isn't good enough. Learn from advice. Look at the story again and see if you can make it more suitable for publication.
- Do make a point of thanking journalists if they've been particularly helpful. The simple courtesy of saying 'thank you' is exercised so rarely that you will stand out amongst the rest.

Advocacy, publicity and tobacco sponsorship of sport

As part of its ongoing battle against the tobacco industry and its sponsorship of sport, the quit smoking organisation ASH (Action Against Smoking and Health) developed this satire on the Winfield Cup Rugby League competition in NSW and attempted to have this placed in *Rugby League Week*, a supposedly non-partisan sport-specific magazine. Complaints by sponsors of the Winfield Cup (Rothmans Pty. Ltd), however, resulted in the ad being withdrawn. The resultant publicity in all the major daily media resulted in ASH's aim (i.e. media advocacy through publicity) being achieved.

Making the big boys pushers

Windfailed Cup

Windfailed Cup

Presented to the NSWRL for services to tobacco companies above and beyond the call of fair play.

When to contact the media

Knowing when to contact the media is crucial. It could mean the difference between a story getting headline coverage, or being hidden beneath other, more 'important' news. For the best chance of getting good coverage the following points should be observed:

1. Plenty of notice should be given, although not too much. A day or two before the event happens is about right.
2. Certain times of the year or week are better than others for getting stories published—for example:
   - Christmas/New Year is a good time, as everything slows down
   - Saturdays and Sundays are often quiet days and good for 'light' stories
   - Sundays are a good day to send out media releases for Monday's news
   - Public holidays are slow
   - Mondays and the day after public holidays give a better chance of getting published
   - Wednesdays and Thursdays are often difficult for daily papers as they're often heavy on content for classified ads (generally Wednesdays) and display advertising (generally Thursdays)
   - Fridays are often the worst day to seek inclusion in Saturday's press
   - Days of highest circulation for daily newspapers are Wednesdays, Thursdays and Saturdays
3. Always look for opportunities to follow up stories by opening up wider issues implicit in the original story and thus make news happen.
4. Although big stories will be taken at any time, there are appropriate times to approach various media, as shown in Table 10.1. Most press conferences or events organised to attract the best possible media attention are organised around 11 to 11.30 am. This gives TV, morning papers, radio and afternoon papers a chance to file their stories in time.

How to contact the media

Ways of contacting the media are also significant for gaining publicity and (more importantly) advocacy over the long term. There are some standard recommendations. For example, *never* write to the editor of a big newspaper or the general manager of a radio or TV station—it's a waste of time. Better means of making contact include:

Telephone

It is quite in order to give a brief message, news tips or invitation to an event by telephone. Longer messages can be faxed to a news editor. Try not to telephone close to deadlines, however, unless it's very important. Be prepared for an abrupt response. Media people operate under excessive pressure and often answer telephones while doing other things.

For best response over the phone:
- Jot down the main points on paper before ringing
- Get the best/most interesting point across first

Table 10.1
When to contact the media

Media groups	Best time to ring	Usual deadlines
Morning papers	Early afternoon (2.30)	1st edn 6–7 pm 2nd edn 10–11 pm Very important news can be later
Afternoon papers	7–8 am	1st edn 9 am Several editions are printed daily
National papers	Morning or early afternoon	1st edn 4 pm
Radio news–ABC	Any time up to 6 pm	Bulletins are broadcast regularly during the day
Radio news—commercial	Breakfast news—5–9 am	Bulletins hourly during the day 10.30–11 am
	Drive-time	3–4 pm
TV news	Morning news bulletins—7–10 am	Morning bulletin 10 am
	Evening bulletin—any time during the morning	Evening bulletin 4 pm

- Elaborate only if asked. If the editor is interested she/he will get a reporter to call back
- Make sure you are available, with facts ready, if someone calls back
- Repeat things if the information is important
- Try not to talk too fast, and pause often
- If you're not sure whether the media will be interested, ask to speak to the staff member who generally deals with reporting on community affairs
- Say up front that you are asking their advice as to whether you have a news item or not
- Find out their deadlines
- If you have an important press release which cannot be delivered or faxed before a deadline, ask to give it to a copy typist

Letter

If the aim is to tell the media about a forthcoming event, it is in order to write a letter instead of sending a press release. Make it brief and give exact dates, times and places. Always give details about where further information can be obtained (e.g. names, telephone numbers, after-hours contacts). Type a letter (double spaced) if possible.

Face-to-face

If a story is very good and a visit is warranted, especially for photographs, ring and make an appointment for an interview. If, because of time constraints, it's not possible to get a press conference organised, choose a friendly journalist to provide the information face-to-face.

Fax

Most messages can be sent to the media these days by facsimile machines (fax). However, because media offices are a hive of incoming information a fax will be lost unless it is specifically directed to a person, and that person is advised it is coming. Newsrooms receive constant worldwide news on cable from news-collection agencies such as AAP Reuters. It is unlikely a small piece from a local health professional will compete with this for press space unless special attention is paid to preparation and direction.

Issuing media releases

MEDIA RELEASES CAN be a simple, but effective way of getting information through to the media. There are some special techniques for doing this most effectively:

- Send material by fax or hand deliver in cases of emergency. Only in cases of dire emergency should a media release be telephoned.
- If additional material is available, send this attached to the back of a media release. *Do not* put back-up material into a press release.
- Be accurate. Media newsrooms can be sued for inaccuracies and if these are found in any media release it will be difficult to maintain credibility with that organisation.
- Don't make statements or claims unless these can be backed up with hard evidence.
- Check all facts, times, dates and places.
- If a particular reporter has been helpful on previous occasions, contact him/her first when there is an event to be covered.
- Put media releases to all media outlets at least one to two days before the event.
- Media releases can be made through agencies such as AAP. These then go to all press from the one source. Check the *Yellow Pages* in the local phone book.

A word of advice: clear your media release and clarify who will be the spokesperson for it through your media officer, if you have one, and then through the highest authorities in your organisation before releasing it to the media. Organisations, both public and private, hate to be embarrassed by media releases which do not reflect the particular organisation's policy on an issue. Also, it is better to be delegated as the contact on the media release by your boss than assume that this is your responsibility.

Writing a media release

- Use the letterhead if possible, otherwise type the full name and address of your organisation at the top.
- Head the sheet 'Media Release' and make sure it is dated.
- Give the release a catchy headline that will attract attention.
- If the article is to be published any time print 'For Immediate Release' underneath the headline. If the release date is some later time, print 'Embargo until (time and date for release)'.
- Put the most important details first (i.e. those most important to the reader).
- Remember KISS (Keep It Short and Simple). Try to keep news releases to one page. Write in short, simple sentences.
- Type all news releases in a standard newspaper-style typeface.
- Use double spacing and one side of the page only, with a 2.5 cm margin on each side of the page.
- Give details, either in the media release or accompanying it, about your organisation, its function and other information of interest.
- Quotations should be attributed to a particular person and not to an anonymous spokesperson who will seem unconvincing to a reader.
- Make sure the person being quoted knows and has given permission.
- For radio or television, put pronunciation of difficult spelling in brackets next to the name or word.
- In general, don't talk about exclusiveness unless a reporter asks for it, and then grant this only after careful consideration. If exclusiveness is granted to a journalist, make sure she/he lets you know when your story is to be used, or if it is to be dropped. In the latter case you are then free to release it to other sections of the media.

What to send with a media release

Since a media release should be self explanatory, a covering letter is usually not necessary. Avoid phrases like 'I hope you will print this' or 'It would be nice to get this published for a change'.

If details of a speech, report, survey or book are being released, enclose the full document. If the document is long, point out the main points to the journalist in the media release. If releasing the text of a speech from which it is suspected the speaker may depart, type 'Check Against Delivery' at the top of the release.

Photographs, sketches or cartoons can increase the chances of a story being run. There are some guidelines for sending pictures with a press release—for example:

- they should be active pictures of people doing things
- they must be of professional standard
- they must be relevant to the main story
- they should be black and white (unless for a colour magazine)

Creating news

The problem of cigarette butt disposal was brought instantly to the public's attention in the early 1980s when anti-smoking activist Bill Snow issued a press release to the effect that he would publicly dump a truckload of cigarette butts into Sydney Harbour on a particular day. The rationale given was that this equalled the number of cigarette butts thrown onto the streets of Sydney that end up in the harbour through the drainage system each day.

The planned event received headline publicity in all major media, and drew an outraged response from the public. Mr Snow, who never really intended carrying out his threat, withdrew the threat, content in the knowledge that he had increased public awareness of the issue.

- they should be gloss rather than matt finish
- they must have a caption typed or pasted on the back naming the people in the photo, what they're doing and where and when
- if a story is about a particular person, a portrait picture can be included with the press release

Letters to the editor

ALTHOUGH LETTERS ARE often thought of as insignificant, the influence of a good letter should not be underestimated. Because a letter is sent does not mean it will automatically be published. Chances of publication can be improved by:

- making letters short, punchy and lean
- making them say something new
- having them signed and authorised by a public figure
- making them amusing—brighten up the readers' day
- writing about a running, topical controversy (make sure though, that you say something new about it)
- showing you're not alone in your concern over the issue
- getting several people to send in their own letter on the same topic; that way at least one might be printed
- if it's a good letter, send it to several papers at once
- not giving up—if you've got something to say and you say it well, then persevere

Staging a media conference

MEDIA CONFERENCES ARE appropriate where wide media coverage is sought for a topical or newsworthy subject. Remember, the notion of a media conference eliminates exclusiveness, so other benefits have to be offered.

- Send invitations one to two days in advance. If possible, send a media release at the same time.

- If an authority is to be interviewed at a media conference, include his/her biography and summary of relevant works with the press invitation.
- Don't assume reporters will have read up on the guest.
- On the day of the conference, follow up the invitation with a phone call to see who is coming. If a particular organisation cannot be represented, explore the possibility of a separate conference for them.
- Make sure the media have prime positions close to a side exit and with close access to phones.
- Make sure there is power available for television crews.
- Providing food and drinks is a nice idea but usually not necessary and never guarantees better reporting. Journalists are busy and can't hang around (unless a story is not meant for immediate news and the press conference is at the end of the working day).
- Helpers should be provided to greet people and distribute press statements; to care for the spokesperson and introduce him/her; to answer questions by journalists; to allow the organiser to move around freely as required.

Media conference format

1. Give a brief background.
2. Introduce the guest speaker.
3. Allow the guest to speak (briefly and to the point).
4. Call for questions from reporters.
5. Allow time for individual reporters to conduct separate interviews—preferably where there are no interruptions.

Writing for media publication

In some instances it is easier for a skilful health professional to prepare an article for publication than it is to attempt to get a story covered by a journalist. This can be a handy source of revenue for the individual or health service and enables the health professional to establish a reputation as a health reporter. Eventually this may lead to newspapers or magazines commissioning the writer to write infrequent articles or features. It is obviously better for a publication to use the byline of a qualified professional on a story rather than that of a generalist journalist.

Generally, the only limiting factor to this is the inability of most health professionals to write entertainingly, but accurately, for popular publications (i.e. their 'translation factor' is low). To do this often requires numerous heartbreaking refusals from editors. It should be remembered, though, that many of the world's best selling artworks and publications were knocked back several times, and who knows how many fine works will remain unpublished (Colleen McCulloch could not interest a publisher in *The Thorn Birds* before she was offered $US1 million for the rights; Van Gogh sold but one painting in his lifetime).

There are a number of steps that need to be learnt by the aspiring freelancer to see him or herself in print:

- Phone first and ask to speak to the editor. Explain your credentials and ask if she/he would like an article on (name the topic).
- Remember an unsolicited manuscript (MS) is not guaranteed to be automatically accepted. It's up to you to make it good enough to sell it.
- If the editor agrees to look at a MS, ask approximately how long this should be (average news stories are 200–500 words; feature articles 1500–2000 words).
- Study the style of the intended publication and lay out your story with similar heading breaks, paragraphs and box inserts.
- Don't ask about money—at least until after the article is accepted. If you are writing for money, make this clear to the editor.
- Prepare the article in double spacing. Give it a provisional title, state the name and credentials of the author and/or organisation and the name of the intended magazine at the top—for example:

FOR: Women's Weekly
FROM: Dr Bill Bloggs PhD, Geriatric Health Adviser
TOPIC: 10 Good Reasons Why Octogenarians Should Lift Weights

- Send the final copy (or preferably deliver it by hand) 'to the person to whom you spoke, marked for their attention.
- Don't ring for at least one to two weeks, unless the article is extremely topical and should be published immediately. Remember, the editor is a busy person and will react badly to constant harassment.
- If the article is rejected, ask politely if there is any problem with your style and how it can be improved, or if the story is too weak.

Tips for making a story newsworthy

- Look for hidden angles to a story.
- Try to say something different.
- Do something visual. Not only does TV news thrive on visual appeal, but a good still photograph makes a journal article come alive.
- Personalise. Specific examples of a problem make much better news and human interest than general comments about the problem by a so-called 'expert'.
- Get quotes from experts, or those affected, where appropriate.
- Bad news can be good news. It is axiomatic that the only really bad news is no news at all. *Any* publicity attracts attention to a project and it is often easier to turn 'bad' publicity into good news than to try and whip up publicity where there is no interest at all.

Ways of using various media for publicity

Radio

Some tips for using radio include the following:

- Radio is instant—use the present tense in news releases.
- The average news item on radio is about five sentences. The average TV item is 1.5–2 minutes. The average radio or TV news interview is less than 30 seconds long.
- If you or your contact feel especially knowledgeable about an area, offer to go on talkback radio.
- Summarise the news in any press release.
- Pick a slack time (e.g. a Sunday) to get news to air.
- If supplying a story to country radio and if your organisation has a good-quality tape recorder, supply your own 'grabs' to the station. First seek advice from the station on how they would like tapes presented.

Tips for radio interviews

- Try to make the listener feel involved.
- Avoid academic language or jargon—speak to the lowest common denominator.
- Ask how long the interview is likely to be and try to finish with a short summary statement.
- Work out in advance your most important points and try to get these across irrespective of the questions asked by the interviewer.
- The technique for good communication on radio is to pretend you are talking to a particular person. Look the interviewer in the eye—even if she/he doesn't sound particularly interested.
- Treat your interviewer as an old friend—call him or her by first name if the chance arises. Also have yourself referred to by your first name.
- Counteract nervousness by speaking slowly and clearly. Don't fidget or swivel the chair because all sounds come across on air.
- If you are asked for information which you don't have, offer to get it and reply without delay.
- Remember, you do not have to answer all questions and shouldn't try to answer questions beyond your area of expertise. The proper response is '. . . I'm not really qualified to answer that . . . ' or 'I'd rather not comment on that . . .'

Television

Television summarises the news in a quick and succinct way. Do not expect to get much time on air—even in country regions—but remember that 'one picture is worth a thousand words'. TV has a much greater impact on the emotions and memory than other media and therefore a brief appearance on TV may be better than a long article in a newspaper (provided the topic and message are appropriate). Television also enlarges mannerisms and flaws and hence should only be used by those confident of their ability to come across well on the medium.

Tips for TV news interviews

- TV news is divided into hard news stories, light stories, sport and weather. There is always a good market for light stories that can be used at the end of the news bulletin or on morning or late-night newscasts.
- Points should be made in short 'grabs' (10–20 seconds) because interviews will invariably be cut and *never* shown in full.
- Don't be intimidated by the interviewer, but also don't try to score points.
- Try not to reply to questions by simply answering 'yes' or 'no'.
- If you feel under pressure, pause and settle in your own mind how you want to respond before you comment. Pauses will generally be cut out.
- If your material is controversial, you can ask to see it and stop it before it is broadcast. But don't abuse the privilege.
- Don't look at the camera or microphone (unless doing face-to-camera monologue). Look the interviewer in the eye.
- After an interview, the camera operator may wish to take a number of camera angles where you are asked not to talk, or to talk about anything. Do as you are asked because these shots will make the story more interesting visually.
- Be prepared. Try not to 'think on the run'. If possible, ask the interviewer before recording what questions she/he is likely to ask and plan short, sharp answers. If she/he is not prepared to supply the questions, at least request the first question that is to be asked. That way you can get a 'warm-up' lead in.
- If you have found that you have said something you wish to withdraw, simply say 'can we record that again? I didn't mean to say that'.

The 'live' studio interview

The 'live' TV interview is probably the most nerve-wracking experience a media novice can have. There is no chance to rerecord, change your mind or explain more clearly. So it has to be *right* the first time.

- If you don't think you will get a fair go, don't appear. If TV appearances are to be a regular thing, get some experience in being interviewed in a recorded situation before you take on the real situation.
- Discuss with the interviewer beforehand the points that are to be discussed, but avoid saying you don't want to discuss a matter—that's an open invitation to bring it up.
- Don't be drawn if you don't want to. Say politely 'I can't discuss that' or '. . . I can't comment on that'.
- Wear 'quiet' clothing but avoid whites and blacks as these can 'glisten'. Stripes and shiny badges or brooches should also be avoided.

Olympians want to CRUSH habit

CONSUMERS ASSOCIATION

Tobacco-aided sports opposed

Sports sponsorship by tobacco slated

SYDNEY. — Sports sponsorship has made a mockery of the 1976 broadcast ban on cigarette advertising, the Australian Consumers Association said yesterday.

The association, publisher of Choice magazine, yesterday launched a new attack on cigarette advertising, calling for widespread opposition and boycotts of tobacco-sponsored sporting events.

A spokesman for the association, Mr Simon Chapman, said smoking was now confirmed as Australia's biggest killer, with an estimated 10,400 deaths each year.

Mr Chapman said it was curious that health sporting activity should be linked with an industry directly responsible for more than 10,000 deaths in Australia annually.

He said the association would be calling for amendments to the Broadcasting and Television Act to prevent "indirect" cigarette advertising.

"In 1976, cigarette advertising was banned from radio and television, yet it has been estimated that in the last summer cricket season, the Benson and Hedges brand name was seen over 40,000 times on the Nine Network alone," Mr Chapman said.

He put much of the blame for cigarette advertising with sporting administrators, most of whom, he said, were business men and entrepreneurs little concerned with the health of young Australians.

Most sporting administrators strongly disagreed with this, favoring instead the argument that everyone should have freedom of choice and that advertising was only directed to smokers and not non-smokers.

On the whole, Mr Chapman said, the sponsoring relationship between cigarette companies and sporting administrators tended to gag any criticism among the sponsored sporting and cultural groups, because you "don't bite the hand that feeds you".

"Many non-smoking sports people

are reluctant to criticise or oppose the association between sport and tobacco, despite an almost overwhelming majority of non-smokers in sporting teams."

Mr Ken Elphik, spokesman for the Sydney Rugby League, said it would make things extremely difficult if Rothmans was outlawed from providing sponsorship funds.

Mr Chapman said this was an indirect effect of tobacco sponsorship, where recipient groups build up a dependency on tobacco money.

"The industry has been able to outbid many competitors and consequently create a dependency by sporting and cultural groups on the large handouts provided," he said.

"Recipient bodies adjust the extravagance of their promotions and events accordingly, resulting in a higher baseline of sponsorship expectations, tending to force out alternative sponsors and certainly Government backing."

Move to boycott tobacco-sponsored events

SYDNEY — Sports sponsorship has made a mockery of the 1976 broadcast ban on cigarette advertising, according to the Australian Consumers' Association.

The association, publisher of Choice magazine, yesterday launched a new attack on cigarette advertising, calling for widespread opposition and boycotts of sporting events sponsored by tobacco firms.

A spokesman for the association, Mr. Simon Chapman, said smoking was now confirmed as Australia's biggest killer, with an estimated 10,400 deaths in a year.

He said it was curious that healthy sporting activity should be linked with an industry directly responsible for more than 10,000 deaths in Australia each year.

The association would call for amendments to the Broadcasting and Television Act to prevent "indirect" cigarette advertising.

"In 1976, cigarette advertising was banned from radio and television, yet it has been estimated that, in the last summer cricket season, the Benson and Hedges brand name was seen over 40,000 times on the Nine network alone," he said.

Mr. Chapman put much of the blame for cigarette advertising on sporting administrators. He said most of them were businessmen and entrepreneurs little concerned with the health of young Australians.

Most sporting administrators strongly disagreed with this, favoring instead the argument that everyone should have freedom of choice and that advertising was directed only at smokers and not non-smokers.

On the whole, the sponsoring relationship between cigarette companies and sporting administrators tended to gag any criticism among the sponsored sporting and cultural groups because "you don't bite the hand that feeds you."

"Many non-smoking sports people are reluctant to criticise or oppose the association between sport and tobacco, despite an almost overwhelming majority of non-smokers in sporting teams," Mr. Chapman said.

"The industry has been able to outbid many competitors and consequently create a dependency by sporting and cultural groups on the large handouts provided."

"Recipient bodies adjust the extravagance of their promotions and events accordingly, resulting in a higher baseline of sponsorship expectations, tending to force out alternative sponsors and certainly Government backing."

The Consumers' Association would call for widespread community opposition and boycotts of tobacco company-sponsored events and start organised picketing of concerts, exhibitions and sporting events backed by tobacco sponsorship.

The association also would call on individuals in sport and the arts to dissociate themselves publicly from involvement in such events.

Mr. Chapman said the action was being taken in direct response to the recent publication of *Don't Sit on the Sidelines*, a book circulated by the Tobacco Institute of Australia Ltd.

The book says sport has been helped financially by the tobacco industry and contains letters of support and thanks to the industry signed by 36 sporting administrators.

Mr. P. Beattan, corporate affairs manager of W.D. and H.O. Wills, which makes Benson and Hedges cigarettes, said the book was a statement of cigarette companies' firm intent to maintain their traditional right to accept or refuse proposals by sporting bodies for sponsorship.

"Equally, it reiterates the principle that sporting bodies have the right to make their own decision in this matter," he said.

"Unfortunately there are those who think they should make the choice for them."

Advocacy as a media objection

- If the interviewer uses a harassing technique, don't respond in kind. It only makes you look bad.
- At the end of an interview you may still be on air. Keep looking at the interviewer and wait until you are sure recording has finished.
- Get as much practice as you can by watching yourself on video and correcting any obvious deficiencies.

Press

Newspaper articles are often cut before publication so do not be surprised to see that what you submitted has been edited.

Interviews

- Avoid saying 'no comment' or refusing to talk to press journalists. Both will hinder further relations with that reporter and publication.
- If you need time to collect your wits, ask the reporter to call back or arrange to call back yourself.
- Don't talk down to journalists.
- Don't underestimate local newspapers. Local papers not only have large circulations, but are also widely read—to the tune of about 92% of the population.
- Send local newspapers regular copies of newsletters, reports, results, speeches . . . anything that may be of interest to residents. Local papers are usually pleased

to have a regular column or correspondent and only need to be approached with an example.

- Local newspapers rely heavily on advertising. Be prepared to pay for advertising space but ask for editorial or other space in return. It is unfair to expect the press to give you free publicity all the time.

Community service announcements

Most radio and TV stations run community service announcements (CSAs) that give free time to charitable or community service groups. The format of these can be gauged by talking to station programmers.

For radio, it is preferable to provide details of an announcement in typed form, openly and evenly spaced so that it is easy to read. Keep the announcement down to 15–20 seconds reading time. Do not supply prerecorded tapes unless: (a) they have been professionally made; and (b) the station has agreed to play your prerecorded tape. Most stations prefer to have a script which each shift announcer reads on air.

To get a CSA run on TV, the station must first agree to run it. This is not easy because TV time is extremely limited and expensive, and each station usually already has a heavy commitment to public service. At least one month's lead time should be given to television stations or two months if the event is near Christmas or New Year.

The content of CSAs is rigidly controlled by government regulations. Content must be cleared with the TV station before an announcement is produced. If a sponsoring organisation is named, this becomes an advertisement and no longer qualifies for CSA time.

To qualify as a CSA, an organisation must be a charitable or a bona fide registered non-profit organisation. All CSAs, like normal commercials, have to be submitted to the Commercial Acceptance Division of the Federation of the Australian Commercial Television Stations (FACTS) for clearance. That body will examine the CSA for such things as timing, sound and good taste.

Organising media events

PUBLICITY EVENTS MAY be designed to put forward a point of view aggressively (e.g. ACTUP demonstrations), to be entertaining, to be controversial or adversarial, to demonstrate or model desired behaviours (e.g. 'healthy' cooking methods demonstrations, celebrities publicly signing a 'pledge' to quit), to promote specific products (e.g. condoms, quit kits) and services (e.g. mammograms, STD tests) or to be educational (e.g. public lectures). Whatever the communication or behavioural objectives for the participants and immediate audiences, a major aim of the event is to attract media attention and reporting. It should be noted that where events are designed to attract large numbers of participants or spectators, advanced publicity or advertising will be required.

BUGAUP: *changing the face of unhealthy advertising*

BUGAUP (Billboard Utilising Graffitists Against Unhealthy Promotions) was an active 'social change' initiating group of the 1980s in Australia. The organisation gained public awareness not only through defacing billboard promotions of unhealthy products, but also by doing this in a humorous way which often tended to reverse the planned message. The organisation also achieved a lot of publicity for its actions when medical practitioners in the group were (often purposely) arrested for breaking the law.

Campaign launches can be effective ways of creating news and attracting publicity. However, because of the difficulty in getting recognition, these have to be increasingly creative to attract media attention, particularly if the subject area is not exceptionally topical or newsworthy. Media launches can also be expensive and may take funding away from other media approaches. If a launch is to work, it should provide good picture or visual opportunities, involve an expert likely to be sought by the media, or centre around the release of a product or service which is novel or innovative.

Another means of attracting publicity often used by organisations with limited funding is the 'staged' media event. The Greenpeace organisation, in particular, has made an art form of this by staging organised commando-style raids on organisations flouting environmental laws, and informing media contacts confidentially beforehand about these so as to guarantee maximum exposure. The BUGAUP organisation (Billboard Utilising Graffitists Against Unhealthy Promotions) was also highly effective in the 1980s in Australia. (See boxed text and photograph above.) The organisation, although controversial at the time, did lead the way in some respects for many innovative health approaches that have since been taken up by the media.

11

Delivering the message through 'edutainment' and other methods

'Edutainment'

'EDUTAINMENT', OR 'ENTER-EDUCATION', refers to the *deliberate* placement of educational messages in media entertainment vehicles such as TV and radio soap operas (primarily), films, popular music, comics, and (to a far lesser extent) in novels and short stories, in order to achieve some defined objective(s). Edutainment uses media entertainment vehicles whose primary purpose is to attract a commercially viable audience and to achieve socially desirable changes in beliefs (knowledge), attitudes or behaviours. The strategy can be likened to, but is far more extensive than, the paid placement of branded products in such vehicles (e.g. Coca Cola signs deliberately placed to be clearly visible in a movie or soap opera).

The edutainment concept is relatively new, at least in terms of formal recognition by social change professionals in developed countries such as the United States and Australia. Although edutainment methods appear to have been used in some Third World countries as far back as the sixties, it was not until the mid- to late-eighties that the concept was applied on a wider scale with the assistance of organisations such as the Johns Hopkins University Population Communication Services and the United States Agency for International Development (USAID) (Coleman & Meyer 1990). The first international conference on the topic ('The Enter-Educate Conference: Entertainment for Social Change') was held in 1989.

The concept of edutainment as a media tool for health promotion, is restricted in this book to applications where there is *deliberate* co-operation between health and entertainment professionals to achieve a particular health objective. This definition excludes what Wallack (1989) refers to as 'disease-of-the-week' made-for-television movies and soap opera episodes, which have covered issues such as AIDS, bulimia, alcoholism, drug addiction, Alzheimer's disease, incest and child sexual abuse, teenage pregnancy and drunk driving. In these cases, the health issues are dealt with primarily because they are topical and controversial or in some other way newsworthy, rather than with the aim of achieving socially desirable effects. While these productions may have been well intentioned, their primary purpose was entertainment. Furthermore, this 'voluntary' treatment of health issues often tends to focus on individual aspects and to ignore important and relevant socio-environmental factors (Wallack 1989).

Edutainment also excludes specific health productions, documentaries and 'docu-dramas' (i.e. dramatised re-enactments) in which education is the primary purpose of the production. In true edutainment, the principal perceived purpose of the production is entertainment, and the audience should (at least initially) be unaware of the attempt to influence them. As usual in such demarcations, there is a grey area between where productions are perceived to be primarily for entertainment and where they also 'carry a message'. In some cases the dramatic presentation is followed by a discussion with the audience on the issue. For example, the play *EscapAIDS*, which is performed in Australian schools to increase students' awareness of AIDS and to teach them how to avoid contracting it, is generally followed by a discussion led by a trained AIDS counsellor.

As currently practised, edutainment varies from country to country, but consists mainly of writing health or other social issues into particular episodes of ongoing serial programs (usually television or radio soap operas). The issue may be dealt with in one episode or continue over several episodes. In some places—for example, India, Mexico, Jamaica and Indonesia, whole soap operas have been written to deal with a number of related issues (Singhal & Rogers 1989; Coleman & Meyer 1990). Television appears to be the most popular medium, although radio is used extensively to reach rural populations in countries such as Jamaica, Kenya and Indonesia, and to promote popular songs that carry a health or social message (Coleman & Meyer 1990).

Tatania and Johnny—Mexican edutainment

Tatania and Johnny were the teenage stars in a campaign in Latin America that used popular music to promote 'responsible parenthood' (i.e. prevent unwanted pregnancy) in teenage girls. Two songs were written, produced and performed to appeal to the 16–19-year-old target group. The songs became 'hits', and the singers became popular with the target audience. Audience understanding of the messages of the songs was rated as 'high'. A similar project in the Philippines (the Lea and Menudo campaign) introduced a telephone counselling service for young people after the songs' popularity was established. The songs were also used as background in radio and TV spots promoting sexually responsible behaviour.

Source: Coleman & Meyer 1990.

A Mexican television producer and director, Miguel Sabido, is credited with establishing the soap opera as a medium for social change. His methods have been studied and adapted to several countries, often facilitated by a strong cultural tradition of story telling as a means of passing on knowledge. Most applications in underdeveloped countries have been directed primarily, but not exclusively, at social issues that influence economic development, particularly family planning. Other topics covered include literacy, vocational training, agricultural methods, child rearing, female equality, and family harmony.

In recent years, the concept of edutainment has been adopted in developed countries such as Australia and the United States. For example, the Harvard Alcohol Project in the United States, launched in December 1987, used a mix of advertising (PSAs), publicity and edutainment to achieve its goals of promoting the 'designated driver' concept (the non-drinking 'skipper' in Australian campaigns), and changing social norms with respect to drinking and driving. The three major television networks in the United States produced and sponsored PSAs promoting the designated driver concept and there was substantial publicity about the project's efforts. Project staff met with over 160 television writers, producers and studio executives, and obtained endorsement of their aims from key professional associations representing actors and writers. As a result of their intensive efforts, treatment of drink-driving issues consistent with the project's aims appeared in 80 television episodes in the next two television seasons (DeJong & Winsten 1990).

In Australia, soap operas have dealt with the following kinds of health issues: AIDS and discrimination against HIV-positive persons, immunisation, alcohol abuse, mental health, sexually transmitted diseases, sports injuries and cigarette smoking.

How soap operas 'work'

THE USUAL PLOT line in soap operas inserts desirable health or social messages in the following way. For a particular episode, the classic ploy is first to establish a strong emotional link between a lead character (e.g. a young boy) and the viewing audience. This link is built slowly and cumulatively, usually beginning with simply liking the character who is good-natured, friendly, physically attractive and with a pleasant outgoing nature. The next step is to reveal that the character has a tragic or unfortunate background, which arouses considerable sympathy from the viewing audience (e.g. his parents are divorced), and that underneath his brave exterior, the boy is faced with an emotional problem or dilemma (e.g. he would prefer to spend more time with his father who appears to reject him anyway—but his mother, because of some physical illness, relies heavily on him for support). The character is then involved in some traumatic incident wherein his life hangs in the balance while the plot is resolved, usually concurrent with his successful recovery. By associating the message with the boy's recovery (i.e. certain beliefs or behaviours must change in the desired direction to ensure a successful resolution of the plot for the lead character), it is hoped that the audience's views will also change in the desired direction (Davern 1990).

Edutainment and role modelling

One of the major aims of edutainment is to provide appropriate positive role models and appropriate positive behaviour change. When actor Lorrae Desmond quit smoking in 'A Country Practice', health authorities capitalised on the opportunity to develop the quit smoking promotion shown below.

Drama versus argument for persuasion

MUCH OF THE rationale for edutainment is based on Bandura's social learning theory (Bandura 1977). It is claimed that viewers will learn appropriate behaviours by observational learning (i.e. modelling). There is evidence that modelling of televised behaviours does occur. However, a comprehensive theory of how persuasion works via entertainment vehicles has yet to be developed. Advertising researchers have proposed that drama is 'processed' differently from lecture or argument approaches to persuasion, and that these differences might offer some advantages to persuasion by edutainment.

Drama, as distinct from argument, has long been a way of getting a point of view across to an audience. The Gospels' parables, street theatre by social action groups, and patriotic propaganda films during the World Wars (produced by both sides), are all examples of attempting to persuade by drama as opposed to argument. Even today, many advertisements attempt to involve the viewer in mini-dramas. Proponents of this approach claim a greater persuasive power than argument. They claim that by drawing the audience into the story, there is little opportunity for counter-argument and hence a greater likelihood of acceptance of the message.

'Argument' involves a straightforward, logical presentation of the message. The information is processed by the audience at a conscious level and in a presumably rational, logical manner, hence allowing for, and even inviting, counter-argument. The classic exposition of this form of persuasion is the debate. Soap-box orators also fit into this category. In drama, on the other hand, the point of view is presented indirectly, and often peripherally to the main message. Processing of the desired message is done unconsciously, hence bypassing counter-arguing.

Deighton, Romer and McQueen (1989), using the three elements of narration, plot and characters, have proposed a continuum of approaches with 'lecture' or 'argument' at one end and 'drama' at the other end (Table 11.1). Lecture consists of narration only, while drama consists of plot and characters only.

Formal educational methods often include elements of demonstration, role playing and active participation. The late Julius Sumner-Miller's physics lectures are an example of using demonstration and story to increase students' involvement with the lecture material and, hopefully, to promote their learning. Psychological studies support the proposition of increased learning and recall when the audience is actively or vicariously involved in the 'lesson'.

Table 11.1
Components of educational approaches

	Narrated?	*Character(s)?*	*Plot?*
Lecture	Yes	No	No
Demonstration	Yes	No	?
Story	Yes	Yes	Yes
Drama	No	Yes	Yes

Which is more effective?

Although a number of studies have investigated the persuasive power of films and other drama-type materials, there has been little research done to evaluate the *relative* persuasive power of the two approaches. Most studies have been concerned with the power of the medium per se, or with message elements that appear to inhibit or facilitate persuasion. One exception to the above, although not in the area of edutainment, is a study of advertising by Deighton et al. (1989). Deighton and his colleagues categorised 600 successful television commercials as either lecture or drama. They found no difference in the mean persuasion scores of the two sets of ads, although their results did show that the two types of ads were processed somewhat differently.

How effective is edutainment?

EVEN THOUGH EDUTAINMENT has been subjected to little formal or adequate evaluation, there is some evidence that this use of the media does have an impact and, because there are few costs involved, it can be cost effective.

Evaluation of edutainment projects has been largely post-hoc (i.e. no benchmark measurements were taken), or has been concerned with process and immediate impact effects (e.g. Blakey & Pullen 1991). In other cases, as with the Harvard project, the influence of edutainment components cannot be separated from the influence of other components. Nevertheless, a number of examples have shown quite dramatic behavioural effects.

A 1969 Peruvian soap opera (called *Simplemente Maria*) told the rags-to-riches story of Maria who sewed her way to socio-economic success with a Singer sewing machine. Wherever the program was televised in South America, sales of Singer sewing machines increased substantially (Singhal & Rogers 1989). Similarly, but on the negative side, graphically described and widely publicised suicides and homicides often are followed by a number of 'copy cat' events (Cialdini 1984).

Regardless of evaluation results, edutainment has clear advantages for presenting potentially threatening or sensitive topics in a non-threatening way, and of reaching people who might otherwise not attend to the message when the source is clearly identified. A possible drawback to edutainment is that writers and producers, ever mindful of their audiences, prefer to emphasise the personal rather than social aspects of disease, to oversimplify or distort complex issues, or to avoid controversial issues altogether.

Implementing edutainment

ACHIEVING CO-OPERATION BETWEEN health professionals on one hand and entertainment industry professionals on the other, requires each to have a good understanding of the other's needs (Montgomery 1990). Health professionals, as the mendicants in most cases, must recognise and appreciate the commercial needs of the producers and the creative needs of the artists. In marketing terms, they must offer these people something in return for their co-operation. Overall, health professionals must accept that their messages must be subtle and secondary to the entertainment aspects, and entertainment professionals must accept that health promotion messages can enhance the audience appeal, and hence the profitability of commercial productions (Coleman & Meyer 1990).

Other ways of delivering the message through the media

THREE MAIN WAYS of delivering a health message through the media have been delineated, but there are a number of other, less commonly used ways of using mass media for health promotion. Some of these are comparatively new, others have been used for some time; all are used relatively rarely, although there are signs that some may become more popular in the future.

The application of edutainment to Aboriginal issues

Given the strong oral history tradition and the use of storytelling to pass on cultural and religious beliefs amongst Australian Aborigines, it is likely that an edutainment approach would be appropriate for this group. Spark (Spark & Mills 1988; Spark et al. 1991; Spark et al. 1992), in an innovative approach to Aboriginal health promotion, used a community development model to elicit 'stories' from Aboriginal communities that contained health messages about issues considered important by the community. Aboriginal artists co-operated with community Aboriginals to express the stories in pictures. These pictures, or parts of them, were then made into posters, or printed onto T-shirts, or developed into TV advertisements and shown on remote television in the Kimberley region. Evaluation of the project indicates a high level of awareness and satisfaction with the approach, although the duration of the program was probably not adequate to allow for behavioural, structural or social change.

---

1. Human interest news items: the 'a su salud' (to your health) program

Human interest news items are an under-utilised media method with potential for local use where media costs and demands on time are not prohibitive. The 'Programa A Su Salud' is a Spanish language mass media program based on Bandura's (1977) social learning theory (Ramirez & McAlister 1988). The Texas-based program attempts to use social modelling to achieve health behaviour change amongst Mexican Americans. The program was initially directed at smoking cessation (in 1985) but has since been extended to other health behaviours. Mexican (or Hispanic) Americans were chosen as the target for the campaign because: (a) they appeared less knowledgeable than other Americans about cancer and heart disease risk factors; (b) there was an increase in tobacco and alcohol advertising aimed at this population; and (c) there was a lack of health promotion campaigns specifically targeting this group. Spanish was the language chosen because many Hispanics have little or no command of English, and even bilingual Hispanics prefer Spanish language media.

A mass media campaign was deemed a necessary and potentially effective component of a health promotion program because: Mexican Americans are less likely to have contact with, and are more suspicious of, health professionals; they are more likely to use mass media as sources of health information than other Americans; they have relatively high exposure to Spanish programming; and preliminary research suggested that such programming could increase knowledge and concern about risks of heart disease (Ramirez & McAlister 1988).

The 'a su salud' program differs from other mass media campaigns in a number of ways. Firstly, it uses role models from within the community in its message design; secondly, there is extensive community involvement in all aspects of the program; thirdly, the mass media components become an integral part of media programming. One or more individuals from within the community are 'tracked' in a series of 5 to 10 minute television programs as they deal with some health issue (e.g. quitting smoking, losing weight, starting an exercise program). The role models discuss what made them change, the skills they used to make the change, and how they felt during and after the change. The programs are produced in a news format and, with the co-operation of the local television station, appear just before the station's news programs. The stations further co-operate by promoting these spots along with their own program promotions. The spots air up to twice a day and on two days of the week, for a month. Different health issues are dealt with each month. The television program is supported by print media. Articles dealing with the health issue appear in the local newspapers.

2. Televised interventions and regular print columns

This type of media use is similar to university of the air courses, or televised cooking, gardening or other do-it-yourself programs. For example, the North Karelia project that targeted the prevention of coronary heart disease, involved the broadcasting of comprehensive smoking cessation programs and other programs concerned with dietary changes on national TV (Puska, McAlister, Pekkola & Koskela 1981; Puska et al. 1985a). These TV programs were preceded and accompanied by extensive community activities. In terms of absolute numbers of quitters attributing their quitting to the TV programs, these programs were considered effective (Puska et al. 1985b).

It is clear that unless a major sponsor (or sponsors) were involved, such interventions would be prohibitively expensive. Hence it is more likely that these interventions will occur only where they can form part of an existing regular program and if the station considers that a program will be of interest to its regular viewers or can attract new viewers. Such an approach can be viewed as a blend of publicity and edutainment. As an example, a popular TV program in Israel followed a quit smoking group over three consecutive programs (the program was broadcast every other Sunday). The quit smoking group was only one segment of the program which generally covered four to five family and household issues such as gardening, home decoration, pets, children and education (Ben-Sira 1982).

Many newspapers and magazines include a regular health feature written by a health expert. The systematic use of such columns has been shown to increase knowledge about health issues amongst readers.

3. Health programming

The production of *one-off* health programs is not new. Documentaries or pseudo-documentaries produced by or for health authorities, or by the news media themselves (with or without the endorsement of health authorities), have been around for some time. The extent to which the news media themselves produce such programs depends on the newsworthiness of the issue—that is, the ability of the topic to attract an audience. Major health crises fall into this category (e.g. tuberculosis, poliomyelitis and, more recently, AIDS).

However, no doubt encouraged by the public's apparent strong interest in health issues, program *series* on health are now being produced for television. The ABC's 'Body Show' and 'Everybody', and commercial programs such as 'Healthy, Wealthy and Wise' and 'Only Human' are examples of this trend. According to Rissel (1991a and b), there is some evidence to suggest that people who watch health-oriented series like this are already interested in health issues and could be described as the 'worried well'. Nevertheless, there is likely to be a flow-on effect of (presumably) accurate health information in the community from the growth in popularity of this type of program. Interaction with an audience (e.g. through a 'Quit and Win' register for smokers (Chapman et al. 1993)) can increase the effectiveness of the approach.

4. Video distribution: Doctors Television Network

The Doctors Television Network (DTV) is a privately owned organisation based in Sydney, Australia. This medical practitioner-owned company places video machines and TV monitors free of charge in GPs' waiting rooms. Participating practices are supplied with a looping (i.e. continuous playing) tape that contains general entertainment material (e.g. travel features), interspersed with program material dealing with specific health issues (e.g. heart disease, its risk factors, and how to minimise risk). Commercial advertising is included on the tape to provide the revenue necessary to support the venture. To date, distribution is limited to a small number of practices throughout Australia. As installation expands, it has the potential of bringing important health information to a captive audience.

5. Educational news

While edutainment attempts to include health messages in entertainment, educational news attempts to deliberately include educational messages in news items. For example, in co-operation with a local newspaper in the United States, the reporting of road trauma was reported in a way that included information from road trauma research and how injury can be avoided. Before and after surveys, following an eight-week trial of the program, revealed significant changes in people's perceptions of road trauma (Wilde & Ackersviller 1981). This method of media use, although not common at present, also presents opportunities for the future and calls for an enterprising approach to health promotion by those professionals working in the field.

The Measures

'MEASURES' REFER TO the means by which a media promotion or campaign is developed, monitored and evaluated. These can range from qualitative (formative), to the more highly objective quantitative (summative) research techniques. Much of the expertise for this has been gained from market research which has well-developed and highly sophisticated measures for carrying out the research procedures referred to in Chapter 12.

Formative measures are generally used to help the formation of a media intervention—for example: market segmentation, target audience selection and description; attitude research and the development of message concepts; pretesting audience reaction to campaign components. *Summative* measures are usually those involved in assessing the outcome or evaluation of a campaign— for example, changes in attitudes, knowledge and behaviour.

Adequate strategy development research and pretesting and pilot testing of campaign materials not only increase the chances that the campaign will be successful, but also assist in assessment if the campaign does not meet its objectives. The more adequate has been the formative research, the more likely it will be that campaign failure was due to factors related to implementation or to other factors not under the control of the campaign managers. In the past, evaluation of media campaigns has suffered from the fact that inadequate formative research was carried out. Unfortunately, some analysts then attributed campaign failure to the unsuitability of the media for health promotion rather than to deficiencies in campaign materials.

Measures of effectiveness in health promotion campaigns depend to a large extent on the point in the hierarchy of effects (discussed in Chapter 3) which has been set as an objective for the campaign. Changes in behaviour may not always be appropriate for media campaigns with limited funding, whereas increases in awareness or knowledge and changes in attitudes might be. Hence the first point in evaluation needs to be a clear re-assessment of objectives. Other tasks of the measurement process, such as those proposed for evaluating AIDS media campaigns (Coyle, Boruch & Turner 1989) are that the desired outcomes be: (1) made more explicit; (2) measured repeatedly; (3) reached (or retargeted) prior to developing further campaigns; (4) monitored periodically to ensure they are maintained once they have been achieved. There are several approaches to evaluation which are the subject of other books (e.g. see Hawe, Degeling & Hall 1990). In Chapter 12 we describe the types of measures most relevant to the development, testing and evaluation of media campaigns.

12

Delineating the measures

P ERHAPS THE MOST useful summary of research methods specifically related to the evaluation of health promotion campaigns is that of the United States National Academy of Sciences (Coyle, Boruch & Turner 1989). Coyle et al. (1989) delineated four types of evaluation: *formative, efficacy, process,* and *evaluation.* These four types of research are designed to answer, respectively, the four questions: What message strategies and materials would work best? Could the campaign actually make a difference if implemented under ideal conditions? Was the campaign implemented as planned? What impact, if any, did the campaign have?

Formative measures: 'What is likely to work best?'

FORMATIVE MEASURES ARE used in the development of media materials and campaigns. These can include quantitative research, such as surveys, literature reviews and epidemiological analysis. However, generally the most valuable formative research uses qualitative measures such as focus groups which not only provide details about the parameters of any target group, but help to identify, shape and assess the potential impact of a message.

Coyle et al. (1989) recommend four processes in the formative stage of a campaign.

1. Idea generation

Once a health problem has been identified and the parameters of this outlined (e.g. through epidemiological observation), the next step is to develop a message that has motivational power. In the case of a campaign designed to reduce abdominal obesity in working men (see information in the box on page 152) used as an example throughout this chapter (Egger & Mowbray 1993), epidemiological data suggested that abdominal obesity is prevalent and a health risk in working men. However, little was known about how men thought, felt or acted in relation to the problem. Focus groups revealed that men were not aware of the health risks, were keen to do something

The GutBuster (abdominal obesity in men) campaign

Sponsoring body: Hunter Centre for Health Advancement and NIB Health Funds.

Background: Almost three out of four men in the Hunter region of NSW were found to have high-risk level abdominal obesity.

Objectives:
1. Increase knowledge of health risks of abdominal obesity.
2. Increase awareness of waist-to-hip ratio (WHR) measures.
3. Increase involvement of men in weight-reduction activities.

Media: TV, radio; local press; posters; information tape, courses.

Market: Lower socio-economic 'weight cycler' males over 35 years with a potbelly.

Message: Abdominal obesity is unhealthy.

Method: Advertising, publicity.

Measures: Over 90% awareness in the community; 15% of households had collected tapes and 9% knew of someone who had tried to lose weight as a result of the campaign.

Source: Egger & Mowbray 1993.

about it once they became aware, but had little information about what to do. The idea generated from this was a campaign to increase knowledge and awareness of health risks associated with abdominal obesity and, given the (latent) motivation to do something about it, to direct men to an accessible program.

2. Concept testing

Concept testing is an iterative process that attempts to determine the relevance and power of an idea among the potential target audience. Many health messages are designed outside the context of the lives of the people to whom the message will be delivered. Testing of the message, usually in a flexible environment such as a focus group, may well lead to a revision or modification of the message which will make it more appealing to the target audience. Testing of the 'GutBuster' idea, for example, led to the understanding that men, whilst not (at least outwardly) motivated by the aesthetic value of reducing weight off their stomach, did have a desire to look trimmer for health and mobility reasons.

Focus groups are also the usual method of concept testing because they allow a greater range of opinions without the defensiveness often generated by personal interviews. However, there may be occasions where group processes can provide barriers to understanding—that is, when behaviour may involve protective actions aimed at presenting an appealing view of oneself in front of a group. In these cases, individual interviews may be more effective. Quantitative survey research is often carried out to confirm that the final concept is acceptable to the total target audience population. Laboratory-style experiments can also be used to test different concepts by exposing different, but matched, groups to different concepts and then comparing the reactions of the two groups.

Focus group measures used at this stage of a campaign also provide ideas about the 'psychographics' of the target audience which aid in the process of audience segmentation. A preliminary profile of abdominally obese men, for example, is shown in the box on page 156. If resources are available, this can be validated at a later point with a more quantitative assessment.

3. Development of communication objectives

The product of the two processes mentioned above is the development of a set of communication objectives—that is, a statement of the knowledge, beliefs and attitudes to be instilled in the target audience in order to lead to the desired behaviour change (see Chapter 7). This then becomes the starting point for the development of creative materials for the campaign. In the case of advertising and publicity, this would form the basis of the brief given to the advertising or public relations agency. Again, using the abdominal obesity example, a set of objectives was developed which led to the design of the 'GutBuster' campaign based around a paper tape with information printed on it for measuring waist-to-hip ratios in men.

4. Copy testing

There are usually several ways of executing the concept or message strategy, and no single approach is the only way. Copy testing is designed to maximise the possibility that the approach taken is likely to be the most effective under the circumstances.

Copy testing involves exposing a test audience to a draft of the message (e.g. an advertisement, press release, pamphlet or video presentation) and evaluating the potential success of that message in achieving the communication objectives. Other focus groups of target audience members are asked to watch, listen to, or read and then discuss media materials as a way of making sure they are understandable and get the message across.

Focus groups should not be used in the final stages of pretesting where a 'go/no-go' decision is required (e.g. whether to launch a TV ad, print a brochure or produce a radio ad) or, as is often the case, in choosing between several different concept executions. If pretesting is required at this stage it should be quantitative because it is necessary to know what percentage of the target audience is unable to understand the message or finds the message not believable, for example.

Quantitative data is required so that performance levels can be set for the media materials. For example, TV ads or brochures should be understood by 90% of the target audience. If only 75% of the target audience understand the ad or brochure and it is costing $100 000 to air the ad, or print and distribute the brochure, then that 25%, or $25 000, is being wasted. Focus groups cannot provide this sort of data. Apart from requiring a projectable quantitative decision, there are other reasons why final campaign materials should not be tested in focus groups (Rossiter & Donovan 1983): the conditions of exposure are unrealistically long and invite members to play the role of 'expert critics'; and individual reactions to materials are prevented or modified by group interaction.

This is not to say that pretesting cannot be carried out on groups of people. It can, and it is often convenient to do so. The key point is that the individual's response is private (e.g. using a self-completion questionnaire) and not a publicly shared one as it would be in a focus group.

Quantitative copy testing involves exposing the material(s) to carefully screened members of the target audience and, where appropriate, comparing their responses to those of a similarly selected control group who are not exposed to the material(s).

Copy testing: what to measure

The following kinds of measures are usually taken after exposing people to campaign materials, although specific measures will vary according to the type and objectives of the material(s):

1. The thoughts and feelings generated spontaneously by the material.
2. The extent to which the message is correctly understood.
3. The extent to which the message is credible.
4. The extent to which the message is seen to be personally relevant, important and useful.
5. The extent to which the message motivates the recommended action.
6. The extent to which the audience see the recommended action as effective and themselves as capable of performing the action.
7. The likes, dislikes and specific confusions associated with the material(s).
8. The extent to which the presenter or models in the materials are credible and relevant as role models to the target audience (where appropriate).

The use of focus groups

FOCUS GROUPS HAVE been mentioned frequently throughout this book and are receiving increasing attention as a research tool for health promotion (Basch 1987; Egger, Donovan & Mowbray 1992). However, the idea is not new. As Morgan (1988) has pointed out, the technique was first discussed in the 1920s (Bogardus 1926), then resurfaced in the 1940s when the persuasiveness of wartime propaganda efforts was examined (Merton & Kendall 1946). More recently, they have been used in a variety of topic areas ranging from quitting smoking to healthy lifestyles and in commercial product marketing with a health education focus (Calder 1977; Rickard 1992).

Focus groups involve in-depth, directed discussion with small, specially selected groups (usually 6–10 people) facilitated by an experienced leader trained in the behavioural or social sciences. Discussions are usually tape recorded and their content analysed for themes, concepts, ideas and hypotheses through a range of analysis techniques (see Krueger 1988).

An important point to note is that focus groups are qualitative in nature. That is, they are not intended to provide quantitative data that can be generalised throughout the total population. The major aims of focus group research are to identify the points of view of a particular section of the population, to understand how these have developed, and to determine how they might be changed. Qualitative research therefore is primarily descriptive, analytical and interpretive. It provides the basis for grounded theory and hypotheses for testing on larger representative samples. Quantitative research determines the extent to which the various points of view identified in the qualitative research exist in the total population and experimental research can be used to test the validity of conclusions drawn from qualitative research.

Focus groups may be a self-contained research method. However, they usually add to, rather than replace other research techniques. An exception may occur if funding and timing are limited and if a lot of statistical information is available about a target audience, and where 'fine tuning' in terms of concept development, targeting or style of presentation might significantly enhance the impact of an intervention.

Focus group processes

The process of running focus groups involves detailed planning and structuring and sensitive, unbiased interpretation. It requires special skills and experience to draw out themes and projections that may arise as part of the dynamics of group processes and to get behind the underlying suspicions and defences of individuals making up the group. If a group facilitator is untrained, the focus group process becomes merely a meeting, with its findings limited to the contributions of a number of de facto 'experts' in the topic. Detailed processes for the running of focus groups are covered in a number of texts including Krueger (1988) and Basch (1987).

A professionally conducted focus group can serve a number of functions including:
- identifying a target audience with the greatest potential for change
- identifying modes of communication
- determining the communication strategy
- identifying concepts for the communication approach
- identifying motivations for, and barriers against change in the target audience

Using focus groups for segmenting abdominally obese men

Market segmentation usually has quantitative connotations, with images of vast amounts of data being analysed to generate the segments. However, segmentations can also be generated from qualitative research. Focus group research was conducted as a preliminary to a weight control campaign for 'blue collar' males in the Hunter Valley region of NSW in 1992. This resulted in a tentative segmentation of the target audience as follows:

	'Cyclers'	*'Perennials'*	*'Deniers'*
Onset of obesity	Late	Early	Late/Early
Predominant body shape	Android	Ovoid	Android/Ovoid
Weight change frequency	Regular	Irregular	Rare
Attitude to weight loss	Positive	Positive but frustrated	Negative
Motivation to lose weight	Feel better/ Family pressure	Fit clothes/ Look better	Health (if any)
Relative ease of losing weight	Easiest	Hardest	Hard
Coping mechanisms	Humour	Resignation	Denial
Apparent group size	Largest	Small	Small

Source: Egger & Mowbray 1993.

Efficacy testing: 'Can it work and can it be improved?'

EFFICACY TESTING INVOLVES testing marketing media materials before finalising them for mass circulation in a campaign. Efficacy testing is usually conducted in a sample of a population with characteristics (e.g. demographics, psychographics) similar to those of the larger target audience. Often, this may be simply a sub-section of the target audience who are exposed to the campaign first, allowing a 'rolling' form of evaluation to be carried out before the campaign is taken to a larger section of the audience.

Efficacy testing is designed to measure whether a campaign *could* work if it was implemented optimally, but under 'real world' rather than laboratory-type conditions. Efficacy testing is carried out through random sample surveys—usually comparing a test with a control area—and limited-scale assessments of measures such as calls to a hot line, sales of associated products and enquiries about courses.

In the commercial world, efficacy testing is frequently carried out through test marketing of campaigns in a limited area so that excessive risk or cost are not involved. The Hunter Valley region of NSW, or Adelaide in South Australia are often used as test markets because of the varied nature of their populations which reflect that of the nation in microcosm. Surveys are carried out (by phone or personally) and sales figures closely analysed in the area during the test period. If results are positive, the campaign may then be taken to a larger test market, run sequentially in different markets or run as a national campaign.

Process research: 'Is the campaign being delivered as proposed?'

PROCESS MEASURES ARE carried out on the content of a campaign either during or at the end of a promotion. The questions these measures are designed to answer are whether the campaign was exposed as proposed, whether the campaign was noticed, and by whom? Aspects of concern are recognition, recall and potential impact of a promotion. Process measures can range from personal interviews to recording of target audience demand for information and materials.

If paid advertising is being used, a media schedule for advertisements will be readily available as a measure of exposure. If PSAs or publicity are the media methods used, it may be necessary to commission audits of exposure—for example, newspaper clippings or radio transcripts. These are carried out commercially by special organisations such as press clipping services, and can be commissioned over the life of a campaign.

A second process measure is the demand for services promoted through media exposure: calls to a telephone hot line; number of public enquiries; 'spin-off' media (e.g. extra publicity generated); sales or requests for products or services. Paper tape measures promoted as part of the 'GutBuster' campaign were advertised as being available free from the offices of a local sponsoring health insurance organisation. In the first four days of the campaign, the initial supply of 11 000 was taken, and an additional 4000 were produced and requested during the next week. For an estimated target audience of about 50 000 overweight men, it was assumed from this demand that the message was being communicated effectively. Behavioural measures such as these are measures both of campaign exposure and the ability of the message strategy to stimulate action. In the latter sense they are campaign 'impact' measures.

A more expensive, but possibly more effective method for measuring exposure is sample surveys of campaign awareness. Telephone surveys can be carried out reasonably cheaply to determine whether a message is being seen and understood. Another common procedure is the 'intercept' or shopping centre survey which allows greater opportunity for measurement of aided recognition as well as unaided *recall* of messages by showing photographs of ads or uncompleted sentences of slogans exposed regularly in a campaign. A mid-campaign intercept survey of 300 people during the 'GutBuster' campaign in the Newcastle region showed that about 90% of those questioned were aware of the campaign, 65% were aware of the main message it portrayed (i.e. the dangers of abdominal obesity) and 13% of households had obtained a free 'GutBuster' measuring tape.

Efficacy testing in health promotion

Efficacy testing is rarely carried out in the health promotion area, usually because of time and budget restraints. However, one example (Siska et al. 1992) involved recruiting people to watch a particular news program on a given TV station for a number of nights. People were randomly assigned to a news program that was to air an AIDS ad a number of times, or to a control program that was to contain no AIDS ads. The viewers were not told the purpose of the research. Pre and post surveys showed a significant increase in the proportion of people in the exposed group spontaneously mentioning AIDS as an 'important national issue', but no such increase in the control group.

Source: Siska et al. 1992.

Outcome research: 'Did it work?'

OUTCOME OR IMPACT measures are designed to assess whether, and the degree to which, a media initiative or media campaign has achieved what it set out to do. Short-term effects are usually called *impact* measures, and include intermediary objectives such as changes in beliefs, attitudes and some behaviours. Longer-term effects are called *outcome* measures. These can be determined by a number of means, each with its advantages and disadvantages. Most require pre and post test measures to evaluate the effect of the intervention.

The outcome effectiveness of many health promotion campaigns in terms of morbidity or mortality may not be known for many years. For example, the outcome of the 'Slip, Slap, Slop' campaigns against skin cancer may take 10 to 20 years to be apparent. Similar statements apply to quit campaigns and lung cancer, and dietary fat campaigns and heart disease. Hence these campaigns should be evaluated in terms of intermediate measures such as beliefs and attitudes; behavioural measures such as sun-protection, presenting for screening, maintenance of non-smoking, and dietary habits; and sales data such as per capita sales of sunscreens, cigarettes, and foods containing a high percentage of saturated fat.

Impact and intermediate outcome measures are designed to inform administrators and campaign organisers whether a campaign had the effect it was designed to have—that is, did it satisfy the communication objectives? The main measures used include:

1. *Survey sampling.* Sampling can be used to get population estimates of attitudes, knowledge and self-reported behaviour. In some cases sampling can also be used to get physical measures (i.e. cholesterol, blood pressure, anthropometric measures). As a cost-saving factor, this can be done as a sub-sample of a larger sample. The pre- and post-intervention sampling evaluation has the advantage of giving population estimates in addition to its validity and objectivity. The main disadvantages are cost, time and resource usage and the difficulties

inherent in sampling procedures (e.g. replacements, interrelationships). Pre- and post-test physical measurement of girth as well as attitude and knowledge measures, of a random sample of men from industries in Newcastle were used to test the outcome of the 'GutBuster' promotion. Measures at the different levels (e.g. attitude, knowledge and behaviour change) are vital for determining any changes in the hierarchy of effects (Chapter 3) that may have occurred and not just the ultimate measures of behaviour change.

2. *Sales auditing.* Sales auditing can often be used where sales of a product are an indirect effect of a projected outcome. In a study carried out on the mid-north coast of NSW, the main intervention objective was to encourage older citizens to eat more high-fibre bread. Sales audits were taken of laxative sales from pharmacies in the NSW town of Harrington and these showed a 50% decline in laxative use over a three month intervention period, accompanied by a 60% increase in bread sales (Egger et al. 1991). Other relevant 'sales' audits, depending on the objectives of the intervention, may be: condom, food, cigarette or liquor sales; fitness centre memberships; or the number of chlamydia or STD tests carried out.

3. *Resource use.* Measurement of action-directed resource utilisation can serve as a proxy form of evaluation where sales outcomes are not relevant to a campaign and the budget doesn't stretch to sample surveys. Examples are: the number of telephone calls to a recorded health message, such as an AIDS hotline; demand for pamphlets or other associated media materials; attendance at cooking classes.

4. *Assessment groups:* A last resort form of evaluation is the group interview if, for reasons of expediency or cost, none of the above measures are possible. As with focus groups, small numbers (i.e. 6–10) of target group members can be asked questions—for example, about behavioural, attitudinal change—over the intervention period and implications (albeit tentative) may be drawn from these results. Because such a sample is not necessarily representative, results need to be regarded cautiously. This is especially so if a group convener (as frequently happens for financial reasons) is the same person who has been involved in developing and running media materials.

Summary

MEASURES ARE REGARDED by some health professionals as an imposition; something that is not really necessary when you know 'deep down' that a campaign works, or is bound to work if given enough exposure. Others, who may not be objectively minded, may feel threatened by the use of techniques involving numbers and statistics. In an era of accountability, however, both of these are naive approaches that will result in limited funding and support over the long term. Ideally, all of the measures referred to here should be used, but at the very least, some (and particularly outcome evaluation) should be built into the development of any media campaign. Measures provide the opportunity for creativity as much as the campaign itself. They are often remembered by funding bodies long after intervention materials are forgotten. Hence measures should make up a significant and non-negotiable aspect of media use in health promotion.

13

Planning health promotion media campaigns: the SOPIE approach

OUR ANALYSIS OF the media has concluded that the media can be effective in some forms of health promotion if exercised in a *careful* and *controlled* fashion, using skills *developed* and *modified* from professional media practices and experience in the field. We have stressed that media are only one strategy in health promotion, but they often constitute an important component of other strategies such as community development and community organisation. Planning involves putting together all those elements of the media mix discussed in the preceding chapters.

Strategic planning

STRATEGIC PLANNING INVOLVES answering three questions:

1. Where are we now? (i.e. an analysis of the current situation)
2. Where do we want to be? (i.e. setting goals and sub-goals)
3. How do we get there? (i.e. developing strategies, methods and tactics)

The usual steps in planning are shown in Figure 13.1:

As shown by the feedback arrows, planning is an iterative process whereby objectives, strategies and methods are continually revised in the light of what is viable, given variables such as the nature and extent of the problem, the nature and accessibility of the target audience(s), and the limitations of financial and other resources.

Planning is also time and resource consuming and, in the haste to (be seen to) 'do something' about an issue, is often done poorly or not at all. Poor planning is probably one of the major reasons why many media campaigns have been deemed to have failed. Donovan and Robinson (1992) list the following strategic planning elements

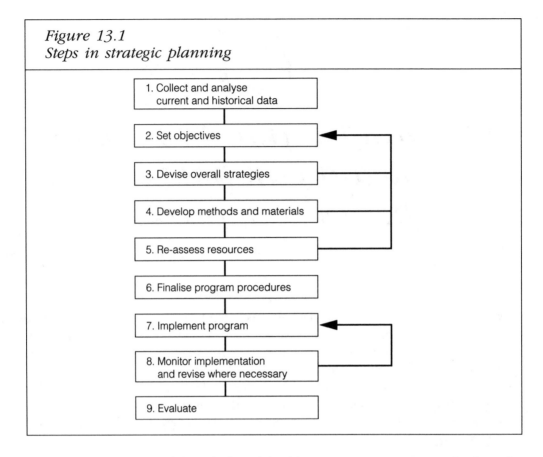

Figure 13.1
Steps in strategic planning

1. Collect and analyse current and historical data
2. Set objectives
3. Devise overall strategies
4. Develop methods and materials
5. Re-assess resources
6. Finalise program procedures
7. Implement program
8. Monitor implementation and revise where necessary
9. Evaluate

that characterise successful media-based health promotion campaigns. The key elements are:

- The setting of overall goals for the campaign and the specification of sub-goals in terms of measurable outcomes.
- The selection and concentration on well-defined target audiences, and identification of specific behaviours required of the target audience to achieve these goals.
- Formative research to understand the target audience: (a) to determine what attitude and belief changes are necessary to bring about the above behaviours; (b) to develop appropriate campaign message strategies; and (c) to pretest various executions of these messages.
- A cost-effective media plan that reaches a maximum target audience with a minimum frequency of exposure, and over a sufficient length of time to achieve the desired communication objectives.
- Evaluation procedures to assess campaign implementation (process research), immediate campaign effects (impact research) and overall goal achievement (outcome research).

- Involvement of all relevant 'stakeholders' in the campaign, and support for the mass media components at the community level.

In this chapter we briefly sum up the processes discussed throughout the book and present the summary in a format that can be used for planning comprehensive media campaigns. The model that we have used is defined by the acronym SOPIE, which stands for:

Situation analysis—identifying the issue; specifying the problem; identifying potential target audiences and strategies; assessing resources; formative research.

Objective setting—defining overall goals and campaign goals; specific behavioural and communication objectives for the target audiences.

Planning—devising message strategies; developing and pretesting materials; selecting media; identifying supporting components.

Implementation—developing detailed program procedures; involving other sectors and stakeholders; program management.

Evaluation—monitoring the campaign; process and outcome evaluation; analysing the problem, the market, the potential strategies.

Situation analysis

THIS STAGE IS intended to identify and accurately represent the extent of the problem or issue and to discover possible causes. It is perhaps the most important stage of any campaign and that which needs the most input. There are four distinct phases:

1. Identifying the problem

Many health promotion programs have been thought out, planned and run without the main problem ever being clearly identified. Problem identification can come from a number of sources including the media itself, literature reviews, epidemiological data, political interest, statistics or public pressure. Data representing the problem are also helpful in selling the program. A further, and important part of analysis, is to determine the timing of an intervention. While there may be a need based on the frequency and severity of the problem, social (and political) attitudes can influence the process of setting priorities in prevention planning. Public acceptance of both the problem and the solution are thus important ingredients for successful intervention. The practical elements of analysis include:

- the nature and extent of the problem (e.g. frequency, severity)
- level of evidence relating to the proposed problem (e.g. will decreasing smoking consumption actually reduce disease?)
- public and political acceptance for (a) the action to be taken, and (b) the proposed action (e.g. would the public accept, and would politicians pay for, a major campaign based on quitting smoking?)

It should be noted that often the problem is not as it seems. For example, early campaigns aimed at reducing smoking were based on increasing knowledge of the health risks of smoking. As these results became understood, it was obvious that the problem was not so much knowledge, but the need to generate feelings of being able to quit and bending to social pressure to quit. Problem identification at this stage showed that programs emphasising the socially unacceptable aspects of smoking were likely to be successful (see box on page 165).

2. Defining the market

Once a problem is identified, there needs to be a clear idea, not only of those for whom the problem is greatest, but also which segments of the target audience are most likely to be influenced, given the available resources. Models of segmentation, such as Sheth and Frazier (1982) and Prochaska (1991), described in detail in Chapter 6, can be used to assist in this process.

Smokers may be segmented on a number of bases—for example, age, sex, length of time smoking, acceptance of health messages, willingness to quit. A segment selected for targeting may not necessarily be the largest (e.g. young women), and different messages will be necessary for different segments.

3. Identifying possible strategies

As noted elsewhere in this book, the media are only one strategy in health promotion. In some cases, the media may be only a minor component of a campaign, or even totally inappropriate. In this stage of planning, the viability of using media is assessed and the role the media are to play, vis-a-vis other strategies, is determined. Furthermore, any comprehensive social marketing program must consider and select other strategies that can add to the aims of the program. This could include changes to the availability of products or materials (e.g. high taxes on cigarettes, restriction of sale to minors) and changes to conditions that encourage smoking (e.g. improvements in the work environment).

4. Generating a strategic concept

Ideas for a campaign concept or major theme are often developed at this stage, using either formative research (see Chapter 12) or skilled assessment by health professionals. A strategic concept is a broad approach to the issue at hand which provides direction for the definition of communication objectives and the development of message strategies. For instance, in the case of skin cancer prevention, a concept may be to encourage greater use of shaded environments. This might then lead on to a strategy of either working with local communities and authorities to provide more shade, or to developing a media campaign to encourage individuals to seek out existing shade. In the latter instance, the concept would be developed fully into a media message.

'Pretty face': the unglamorous side of smoking

Topic: Smoking amongst females.

Sponsoring bodies: NSW Department of Health, Victorian Anti-Cancer Council, WA Department of Health.

Background: Research in the 1980s showed that while smoking rates among males were decreasing, rates were continuing to rise in young females. This was largely because of advertising denoting smoking as 'glamorous'.

Objectives:
1. Change attitudes of females to smoking by making this appear 'unglamorous'.
2. Reduce smoking rates in women.

Media: TV; press.

Market: Females aged 18 to 24, with possible secondary target under the age of 18.

Message: Smoking is ugly.

Method: Advertising.

Measures: Strong opposition from the tobacco lobby. Similar approaches accentuating the effects of smoking on the breath, looks and physical and sexual prowess have no doubt contributed to the declining image of smoking in Western societies.

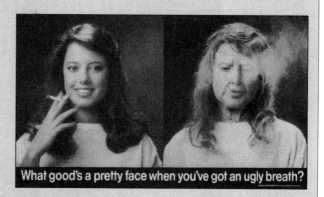

What good's a pretty face when you've got an ugly breath?

Objective setting

BASED ON THE identified problem and the selection of target audiences, the next step is to set overall goals for the campaign and specific behavioural and communication objectives for each target group, as described in Chapter 2 (the Rossiter six-step model).

1. Defining goals

Goals help to determine the direction of an intervention and set out what the program hopes to achieve. Goals are written as broad general statements of objectives. An example, concerned with sexually transmitted diseases, is: 'To decrease infertility due to STDs'. Because they are broad and general, goals do not specify the method of intervention. Hence they need to be accompanied by measurable objectives.

2. Setting objectives

The planning stage is designed to provide a blueprint for action. As part of this, there needs to be a set of clear-cut objectives. Ideally, the objectives of a well-planned campaign should be specific, time-related and measurable. These can be defined in terms of the ultimately desirable outcome (e.g. reduced morbidity) or in terms of intermediate objectives, such as: target population knowledge, attitudes and behaviours; changes in the physical environment; public policy or practice related to health. These are therefore called *outcome* objectives. In the case of motor vehicle injuries, outcome objectives of a preventive initiative may be reduced fatalities, but intermediate measures such as a reduction in driver blood alcohol levels, or even reduction of alcohol consumption in a targeted area, could also be an outcome objective.

As noted previously, individual campaign objectives must be realistic. What can be achieved by one limited-duration campaign must not be confused with what it is hoped to achieve by a series of campaigns and a combination of strategies that would be part of a long-term program.

Planning

ONCE THE DETAILED objectives have been set, the next step is to develop the specific campaign components as outlined in Chapter 2 (the six-step model) and in Chapters 5 and 7 (media and message). The viability and affordability of the different media methods need to be assessed; message strategies need to be identified and executed in various campaign materials; primary and secondary media need to be selected; monitoring and evaluation procedures must be specified; pretesting should be undertaken where necessary; and other non-media components devised. The role of other sectors needs to be defined and their co-operation sought. Adequate resources must be prepared to meet the expected response to the campaign (e.g. child abuse deterrent campaigns inevitably also result in a large number of abused persons seeking counselling).

1. Choosing the method

The method of delivery of a message will depend on a number of factors. Advertising is expensive, but allows full control over message exposure and greater flexibility in presentation; publicity is relatively inexpensive, but depends to a great extent on the 'newsworthiness' of a topic; edutainment is even less able to be controlled by the message initiator and is likely only to work over the long term. Choice of method also depends on the target audience, the campaign objectives and the budget, as well as the skills of the health team.

Primary and secondary media should also be identified and, in the case of advertising, media schedules developed to provide optimal coverage. Where advocacy is the desired outcome, media should be identified for targeting to get the desired message across. The marketing mix also involves consideration of the four Ps of influence: *product, price, place* and *promotion* (Kotler 1989; Novelli 1984).

2. Developing the message

Message development, as pointed out in Chapters 8 and 9, involves firstly, determining the right message to communicate and secondly, designing this in a way that is likely to be most effective. Given a behavioural or attitudinal objective, developing a message strategy attempts to answer the question: what sort of motivations must be aroused, or what sort of beliefs need to be established in the target audiences' minds, to bring about these behavioural or attitudinal changes? The primary tools for message strategy development (i.e. getting the right message) are qualitative research techniques such as individual in-depth interviews, and focus group discussions with members of the target audience.

The message strategy should include the following elements, although not always in each individual message execution:

1. The benefits promised by adopting the recommended behaviour or attitude (i.e. the motivational component).
2. Specific actions that the individual can undertake, whether intermediate (e.g. call a hotline) or related to the desired end-behaviour.
3. Reassurances that the recommended course of action does work.
4. Reassurances that the individual is capable of carrying out the recommended course of action (with appropriate assistance where relevant).

For the message to be executed effectively it should:

- be credible
- be understood and correctly communicate the strategy
- use a language and style appropriate to the attitudes, values and lifestyles of the target audiences
- be clear and unambiguous
- focus on one main message or related set of messages
- be presented in a way that is appropriate to the media method, and to the media and media vehicles in which it is to be placed.

Where more than one method is used, for example, both advertising and publicity (and this should usually be the case), the relative roles of the methods needs to be established and the messages for each developed with these different objectives in mind. Similarly, where different media are used, regardless of method, the characteristics of the media need to be taken into account when developing messages to meet the objectives (e.g. sound effects can be used to enhance message takeout in TV and radio, but not in print; pictorial demonstrations can be used in print and TV, but not on radio).

According to Novelli (1984), the message objective should contain four elements:

1. The benefits the individual can expect (e.g. longer life, cleaner breath).
2. Reasons why the individual should believe the message (e.g. evidence from other ex-smokers).
3. Specific action the individual is expected to undertake (e.g. call the quit line; sign a contract).
4. The tone, or image to be conveyed (e.g. serious, medical, light-hearted).

The message objective should serve as a reference for measuring the effectiveness of communication. For example, if the message is to decrease smoking and thus make people feel better, measures of well-being can be included in the campaign evaluation.

3. Testing the message

Before full-scale implementation of a campaign, media messages should be pretested. The means of doing this are considered in Chapter 12 and include concept testing and efficacy testing. Pretesting messages at this stage can provide direction for improving the message or identifying which of several alternative executions has the greatest potential. Models are available for this stage of planning, including the guidebook on *Pretesting in Health Communications* produced by the National Cancer Institute (1982).

Implementation

IMPLEMENTING THE CAMPAIGN includes setting process objectives (i.e. what is to be accomplished, by whom and when), managing the implementation process (i.e. co-ordination, media liaison, intersectoral liaison), monitoring the process, and being prepared for any negative responses to the campaign.

Process objectives detail the level of activities designed to produce the desired outcomes. They describe the relationship between a project's activities and the desired outcomes. Process objectives are thus not simply lists of activities, but are quantifiable and measurable statements of what the campaign will have accomplished by certain dates. In the motor vehicle injury example discussed above, process objectives would include such things as the number of CSAs to be aired by a certain date and the number of press releases to have been issued by that date, but also could include an awareness by that date, among a specific proportion of the target population, of the consequences of drinking and driving.

Some media campaigns involve a staged 'rollout' of communication materials. The first stage of an anti-smoking implementation, for example, may concentrate on an increased knowledge of less well-known risks (e.g. passive smoking). A second and later stages may be designed to increase pressure on workplace managers, urging them to avoid the risk of litigation from those affected by passive smoking by banning smoking in certain areas of the workplace. Media campaigns in 'new' areas, where knowledge and awareness is low, often aim the first phase of a campaign at educating (or informing) about the problem, then run a second stage to motivate (or persuade) people to do something about this. Advocacy for an issue often follows the increased awareness created by advertising or publicity, as has been demonstrated with regard to smoking.

Monitoring of the program is important in the implementation stage to ensure that the message is getting through to the target audience, and to evaluate the process of operation. This is often done through a recording of requests received about the program. Enquiries for further information, increased demand for quit smoking courses, or increases in the sales of nicotine chewing gum, for example, may be indirect measures of whether the message is reaching and impacting its target audience.

It should also be recognised that there are often vested interests opposed to intervention methods that seek to alter the status quo, and that reaction from these opponents is likely to come at the implementation stage of any campaign. Cigarette and alcohol manufacturers form powerful lobby groups against the introduction of campaigns designed to reduce smoking and drinking, and the Sporting Shooters Association is able to thwart most attempts at gun control advocacy, despite the fact that firearms are a chief cause of intentional and unintentional homicide.

If possible, these contingencies should be considered in the planning stages and approaches developed for coping with them as they arise. Most advertising has to conform to certain regulations (often voluntary codes) and these can be used by vested interests against health authorities that may be sufficiently alert to the processes. Television advertisements, for example, are under the control of the Federation of Australian Commercial Television Stations (FACTS). Cigarette manufacturers have been known to prevent anti-smoking commercials from being aired if these have made statements that cannot be strictly proved about the adverse effects smoking has on health. In some cases, this has been used by health professionals to create publicity around a promotion to ensure that it achieves a wider exposure than might otherwise have occurred. Non-smoking groups, like ASH, are particularly skilful in creating publicity from their promotions by antagonising manufacturers.

Evaluation

EVALUATION INVOLVES A systematic assessment of the degree to which an intervention is meeting its objectives. If the budget allows, this should be carried out midway through a campaign to correct any deficiencies or to capitalise on any new opportunities that present themselves, as well as at the end of the program. Methods of carrying out process, impact and outcome evaluation were discussed in Chapter 12.

In general, evaluation measures should be in place before a campaign is aired. However, in some circumstances, changes in events as a result of the intervention may lead to a modification of the information required. If monitoring shows a disappointing response to the media messages, for example, there may be a need to institute measures to find out why this is so. The lack of response by smokers to a 'Quit and Win' campaign in NSW, which offered the possibility of winning a car, led to the need to

Table 13.1
Planning outline: the SOPIE approach

Stage	Requirements	Processes
1. Situational Analysis		
Problem identification	What is the main issue to be addressed?	Epidemiology, observation, public pressure, press reports
	How strong is the evidence (a) for its existence, and (b) for intervention effects?	
Market identification	Who are the primary target audience?	Epidemiological data, literature review, surveys, focus groups
	Which segments are largest/most likely to be influenced?	
	What are their characteristics?	
Assessment of strategies	Are media justified?	Cost-effectiveness analysis, expert advice
	Are there more cost-effective alternatives?	
Concept development	What is the best general approach of the campaign?	Qualitative research, surveys, situation spotting, informed opinion
2. Objective Setting		
Definition of goals	What are the broad goals?	Consultation
Set objectives	What are the specific objectives?	Consultation
	How are these expressed in measurable terms?	
3. Planning		
Choosing the method	What is the primary method to be used?	Consultation, expert advice, market analysis (e.g. focus groups)
	How can other methods complement this?	
Development of the message	What is the context of the message?	Expert advice, contract services
	Who will develop the message?	
Testing the message	Does the message have the desired effect on a test audience?	Test marketing, surveys, interviews, focus groups
	Can the message be modified to improve its effect?	

(continued)

Table 13.1 *(continued)*
Planning outline: the SOPIE approach

Stage	Requirements	Processes
Selection of media	Which primary media are to be used? Which secondary media are to be used?	Expert advice, target groups assessment (e.g. focus groups)
4. Implementation	What are the process objectives? What monitoring can be done? What provision has been made for coping with adverse reactions?	Telephone interviews, sales audits, information requests
5. Evaluation	What measures are to be used? Did the program reach its intended audience? Did it achieve its objectives? How could it be made better?	Pre and post test, intercept surveys, phone surveys, sales measures, impact and outcome assessments

form some quick focus groups with smokers to redefine the campaign midway through a paid media schedule (Chapman et al. 1993). The focus groups showed that although the competition was well received by non-smoking family and friends of smokers, smokers in 1992 felt besieged by anti-smoking warnings and pressure. Although desperately wanting to quit, many had tried and failed and did not wish to be reminded of the fact—even given the (remote) possibility of winning a car. The message therefore needed to be changed so that it involved more smokers' non-smoking contacts.

Evaluation is often thought of as a luxury in media campaigns where the political imperative is simply to *be seen* to be doing something for the good of the voters. Funding for evaluation is frequently not included in budgets handed down by those who do not understand the evaluation process. However, it is often these same funding sources (e.g. politicians) who use evaluation results to either confirm or deny the value of their funding allocations when these are put under scrutiny. Funding for evaluation should be seen as an integral part of any media promotion, making up sometimes 5–10% of the total budget.

Summary

MASS MEDIA CAMPAIGNS to promote health do work. Their effectiveness, however, depends on the level of skill, experience and judgment that can be put into them, together with knowledge about what has and has not worked in the past. Media methods can vary, and the social and political implications of using one or other of these has been, and is likely to be, an issue for health promotion professionals to wrestle with in the future. As populations increase and technology improves, there is no denying the increasing and all-pervasive nature of the mass media in our lives. To suggest that this has no influence on the way people choose to live their lives, the decisions they make and the attitudes they form is to take a Luddite approach to the study of communications. Mass media not only *can* be used for the social good—that is, to promote health—but also there is a case to suggest they *must* be used if modern societies are not to be denied the right to the information which health and scientific experts are charged with discovering and disseminating.

Bibliography

Acquaviva, F.A. & Malone, R.A. 1981, *The Power of Positive Persuasion: A Professional's Guide to Communications*, Ramsco Publishing, Maryland.

Alderson, W. 1957, *Marketing Behavior and Executive Action*, Irwin, Homewood, Illinois.

Adams, J.R. 1977, *Media Planning*, Business Books, London.

Advertising Federation of Australia 1991, 'Road safety: the Transport Accident Commission campaign in effective advertising', *Casebook of the AFA Advertising Effectiveness Awards 1990*.

Advocacy Institute 1989, *Smoking Control Media Advocacy Guidelines*, National Cancer Institute, National Institute of Health, Bethesda, Maryland.

Aitken, P.P., Leather, D.S., O'Hagan, F.J. & Squair, S.I. 1987, 'Children's awareness of cigarette advertisements and brand imagery', *British Journal of the Addictions*, vol. 82, pp. 615–22.

American Marketing Association Committee on Definitions 1960, *Marketing Definitions: A Glossary of Marketing Terms*, American Marketing Association, Chicago.

Amos, A. 1986, 'British women's magazines—a healthy read?' in Leather, D.S., Hastings, G.B. & O'Reilly, K. (eds), *Health Education and the Media II*, Pergamon Press, Oxford.

Atkin, C. 1981, 'Mass media information campaign effectiveness' in Rice, R.E. & Paisley, W.J. (eds), *Public Communication Campaigns*, Sage Publications, San Francisco.

Atkin, C. 1979, 'Research evidence on mass mediated health communication campaigns' in Nimmo, D. (ed.), *Communication Yearbook III*, Transaction Books, New Brunswick, N.J.

Atkin, C. 1985, *Effects of the Mass Media*, Holt, Rhinehart & Winston, New York.

Australian Bureau of Statistics 1990, *Expectations of Life*, ABS, Sydney.

Australian Consumer's Association 1982, 'The truth about TV ads', *Choice*, May, Sydney.

Australian Institute of Health 1992, *The Health of Australia*, AGPS, Canberra.

Azjen, I. & Fishbein, M. 1980, *Understanding Attitudes and Predicting Social Behaviour*, Prentice Hall, Englewood Cliffs, N.J.

Bagozzi, R.P. & Warshaw, P.R. 1990, 'Trying to consume', *Journal of Consumer Research*, vol.17, pp. 127–40.

Bailey, L. & Haslam C. 1984, *Coronary Heart Disease: Plans for Action*, Pittman, London.

Baker, S. 1972, *The Complete Stylist*, Thomas Crowell & Co., New York.

Bandura, A. 1977, 'Self efficacy: toward a unifying theory of behaviour change', *Psychological Review*, vol. 84, pp. 191–215.

Bandura, A. 1977, *Social Learning Theory*, Prentice Hall, Englewood Cliffs, N.J.

Bandura, A. 1986, *Social Foundations of Thought and Action: A Social Cognitive Theory*, Prentice Hall, Englewood Cliffs, N.J.

Basch, C.E. 1987, 'Focus group interview: an underutilised technique for improving theory and practice in health education', *Health Education Quarterly*, vol. 14, pp. 411–48.

Bauer, R. 1964, 'The obstinate audience: the influential process from the point of view of social communication', *American Psychologist*, vol. 19, pp. 319–28.

Bednall, D. 1992, *Media and Immigrant Settlement*, AGPS, Canberra.

Belch, G.E. & Belch, M.A. 1990, *Introduction to Advertising and Promotion Management*, Irwin, Homewood, Ill.

Ben-Sira, Z. 1982, 'The health promoting function of mass media and reference groups: motivating or reinforcing of behaviour change', *Social Science Medicine*, vol. 16, pp. 825–34.

Better Health Commission, 1985, *The Role of the Media in Promoting Health*, vol. 3, AGPS, Canberra.

Bevins, J. 1987, Using advertising to sell and promote health and healthy products. Paper presented to ACHPER Health Products and Services Marketing Seminar, December, Kuring-gai College, Sydney.

Bevins, J. 1988, Third National Drug Educators' Workshop Proceedings, vol. I, West Australian Department of Health.

Blakey, V. & Pullen, E. 1991, ' "You don't have to say you love me": an evaluation of a drama-based sex education project for schools', *Health Education Journal*, vol. 50, pp. 161–5.

Blane, H.T. & Hewitt, L.E. 1980, 'Alcohol, public education and mass media: an overview', *Alcohol, Health and Research World*, Fall, pp. 2–16.

Bloom, P.N. & Novelli, W.D. 1981, 'Problems and challenges of social marketing', *Journal of Marketing*, vol. 45, pp. 79–88.

Bogardus, E.S. 1926, 'The group interview', *Journal of Applied Sociology*, vol. 10, pp. 372–82.

Bogart, L. 1990, *Strategy in Advertising: Matching Media and Messages to Markets and Motivations*, NTC Business Books, Lincolnwood, Ill.

Bonaguro, J.A. & Miaoulis, G. 1983, 'Marketing: a tool for health education planning', *Health Education*, Jan–Feb, pp. 6–11.

Borland, R., Hill, D. & Noy, S. 1990, 'Being SunSmart: changes in community awareness and reported behaviour following a primary prevention program for skin cancer control', *Behaviour Change*, vol. 7, no. 3, pp. 126–35.

Brehony, K.A. 1971, *Marketing Health Behaviour*, Plennum Press, New York.

Bretz, R.A., *Taxonomy of Communication Media*, Educational Technology Publications, New Jersey.

Budd, J. & McCron, R. 1981, 'Health education and the mass media: past, present and potential', in Leathar, D.S. Hastings, G.B. & Davies, J.K. (eds), *Health Education and the Media*, Pergamon Press, Oxford.

Calder, B.J. 1977, 'Focus groups and the nature of qualitative research', *Journal of Marketing Research*, vol. 14, no. 3, pp. 353–64.

Centre for Behavioural Research in Cancer 1992, Health warnings on cigarette packs. Unpublished report, Victorian Anti-Cancer Council, Melbourne.

Chapman, S. & Egger, G. 1980, 'Forging an identity for the non-smoker: the use of myth in health promotion', *International Journal of Health Education*, supplement to vol. XXII, no. 3.

Chapman, S. & Egger, G. 1983, 'Myth in cigarette advertising and health promotion', in Davis, H. & Walton, P. *Language, Image, Media*, Basil Blackwell, Oxford.

Chapman, S., Smith, W., Mowbray, G. & Egger, G. 1993, ' "Quit and Win" smoking cessation contests. How should effectiveness be evaluated?', *Preventive Medicine*.

Cialdini, R.B. 1984, *Influence: The New Psychology of Modern Persuasion*, Quill, New York.

Cialdini, R.B. 1989, 'Littering: when every litter bit hurts', in Rice, R.E. & Atkin, C.K. (eds), Public Communication Campaigns, Sage Publications, San Francisco.

Coleman, P.L. & Meyer, R.C. (eds) 1990, Proceedings from the Enter-Educate Conference: Entertainment for Social Change. Johns Hopkins University Center for Communication Programs, Baltimore, Maryland.

Coli, T. 1990, 'Eat Less Fat': Results of a Western Australian Campaign. Paper presented to the Australian Association of Health Promotion Professionals, 1989, Melbourne.

Collins, L. 1989, 'An evaluation of leaflet inserts in the local paper as a health promotion activity', in Miller, M. & Walker, R. (eds), *Health Promotion: The Community Health Approach*, Australian Community Health Association, Sydney.

Cook, T.D., Kendierski, D.A. & Thomas, S.V. 1983, 'The implicit assumptions of television research', *Public Opinion Quarterly*, vol. 47, pp. 161–201.

Coyle, S.L., Boruch, R.F. & Turner, C.F. (eds) 1989, *Evaluating AIDS Prevention Programs*, National Academy Press, Washington, DC.

Crask, M.R. & Reynolds F.D. 1980, 'Print and electronic cultures', *Journal of Advertising Research*, vol. 20, no. 4, pp. 47–51.

Cummings, K.M., Becker, N.H. & Maile, N.C. 1980, 'Bringing the models together: an empirical approach to combining the variables used to explain health actions', *Journal of Behavioural Medicine*, vol. 3, no. 2, pp. 123–45.

Davern, J. 1990, 'Promoting the compliance message in a popular drama series'. Conference paper, Public Health Association of Australia, Canberra.

Davidson, W.P. 1983, 'The third person effect in communication,' *Public Opinion Quarterly*, vol. 47, pp. 1–15.

De Musis, E.A. & Miaoulis, G. 1988, 'Channels of distribution and exchange concepts in health promotion', *Journal of Health Care Marketing*, vol. 8, pp. 60–8.

Deighton, J., Romer, D. & McQueen, J. 1989, 'Using drama to persuade', *Journal of Consumer Research*, vol. 16, pp. 335–43.

DeJong, W. & Winsten, J.A. 1990, 'The use of mass media in substance abuse prevention', *Health Affairs*, Summer, pp. 30–46.

Deutsch, R. 1981, *Nuts Amongst the Berries*, Sage Publications, San Francisco.

Di Clemente, C.C., Prochaska, J.A., Fairhurst, S.K., Velicer, W.F., Velasquez, M.M. & Rossi, J.F. 1992, 'The process of smoking cessation: an analysis of precontemplation, contemplation and preparation stages of change', *Journal of Consulting and Clinical Psychology*, vol. 59, pp. 295–304.

Dommermuth, W.P. 1989, *Promotion: Analysis, Creativity, and Strategy*, Piers-Kent, Boston.

Donohew, L. 1990, 'Public health campaigns: individual message strategies and a model', in Bray, E.B. & Donohew, L. (eds), *Communication and Health: Systems and Applications*, Erlbaum, Hillsdale, N.J.

Donovan, R. & Owen, N. 1993, 'Social marketing and mass intervention', in Dishman, R.K. (ed.), *Exercise Adherence:*

Implications for Public Health, 2nd edn, Human Kinetics, Illinois.

Donovan, R.J., Fisher, D.A. & Armstrong, B.K. 1984, 'Give it away for a day: an evaluation of Western Australia's first smoke free day', *Community Health Studies*, vol. 8, pp. 301–6.

Donovan, R.J., Jason, J., Genty, E. & Calcough, G. 1992, 'Using continuous tracking to evaluate the American response to AIDS campaign', CDC report, Atlanta.

Donovan, R.J. & Leivers, S. 1993, 'Using paid advertising to change racial stereotype beliefs', *Public Opinion Quarterly*.

Donovan, R.J. & Francas, M. 1990, 'Understanding communication and motivation strategies', *Australian Health Review*, pp. 103–14.

Donovan, R.J. 1987, 'Evaluation of the national campaign against drug abuse', West Australian Report to the Department of Health.

Donovan, R.J. 1991, 'Public health advertising: execution guidelines for health promotion professionals', *Health Promotion Journal of Australia*, vol. 1, pp. 40–5.

Donovan, R.J. & Robinson, L. (1992), 'Using mass media in health promotion: the West Australian Immunisation Campaign', in Hall, R. & Richters, J. (eds), *Immunisation: The Old and The New*, Public Health Association of Australia, Canberra.

Donovan, R.J, Jason, J., Gibbs, D.A. & Kroger, F. 1991, 'Paid advertising for AIDS prevention—would the ends justify the means?', Public Health Reports, vol. 106, pp. 645–51.

Drew, L. 1982, *The Media: A Guide for Health Workers*, Commonwealth Department of Health, Canberra.

Edgar, T. Freimuth, V.S. & Hammond, S.L. 1988, 'Communicating the AIDS risk to college students: the problem of motivating change', *Health Educ. Res.*, vol. 26, pp. 23–7.

Egger, G. 1991, 'The contributions of prevention to changing health status of Australians since 1960'. Report for the NSW Better Health Program, NSW Department of Health, Sydney.

Egger, G., Wolfenden, K., Mowbray, G. & Peres, J. 1991, 'Bread. It's a great way to go', *Medical Journal of Australia*, 1991.

Egger, G. 1985, 'Health Promotion', in King, N. & Remini, A. *Behavioural Sciences in Health*, Macmillan, Melbourne.

Egger, G. 1989, 'Youth campaign concept testing'. Report to the South Australian Drug and Alcohol Services Commission, Adelaide.

Egger, G., Donovan, R.J. & Mowbray, G. 1992, 'The use of focus groups in nutrition education', *Viewpoint. Australian Journal of Nutrition and Dietetics*, vol. 49, no. 2, pp. 64–5.

Egger, G., Donovan, R.J. & Spark, R. 1990, 'A component circuit approach to needs assessment and strategy selection in health promotion', *International Journal of Health Promotion*.

Egger, G., Fitzgerald, W., Frape, G., Monaem, A., Rubinstein, P., Tyler, C. & Mackay B. 1983, 'Results of a large scale media anti-smoking campaign in Australia: the North Coast Healthy Lifestyle Programme', *British Medical Journal*, vol. 287, pp. 1125–287.

Egger, G. & Mowbray, G. 1993, 'A qualitative assessment of abdominal obesity in working men', *Australian Journal of Nutrition and Dietetics*, vol. 50, no. 1.

Egger, G., Spark, R. & Lawson, J. 1990, *Health Promotion Strategies and Methods*, McGraw-Hill, Sydney.

Elliot, B. 1988, 'The development and assessment of successful campaigns'. Education co-ordinators' workshop on media skills, Brisbane.

Festinger, L. 1957, A Theory of Cognitive Dissonance, Stanford University Press, Stanford, CA.

Fine, S.H. 1990, *The marketing of ideas and social issues*, 2nd edn, Praeger, New York.

Fischer, P.M., Richards, J.W., Berman, E.J. & Krugman, D.M. 1989, 'Recall and eye tracking study of adolescents viewing tobacco advertisements', *Journal of the American Medical Association*, vol. 261, pp. 84–9.

Fishbein, M. & Ajzen, I. 1975, *Belief, Attitude, Intention and Behaviour: An Introduction to Theory and Research*, Addison-Wesley, Reading, MA.

Fishbein, M. Middlestadt, S. & Hitchcock, P.J. 1991, 'Using information to change sexually transmitted disease-related behaviours: an analysis based on the theory of reasoned action', in Wasserheit, J.N., Aral, S.O. & Holmes, K.K. (eds), *Research Issues in Human Behaviour and Sexually Transmitted Diseases in the AIDS Era*, American Society for Micro-Biology, Washington, DC.

Flay, B.R., DiTecco, D. & Schlegel, R.P. 1980, 'Mass media in health promotion: an analysis using an extended information-processing model', *Health Education Quarterly*, vol. 7, pp. 127–48.

Flay, B.R. 1987, 'Mass media and smoking cessation: a critical review', *American Journal of Public Health*, vol. 77, no. 2, pp. 153–60.

Flesch, R.F. 1946, *The Art of Plain Talk*, Harper and Row, New York.

Flesch, R.F. 1947, 'How to write copy that will be read', *Advertising and Selling*, March, vol. 113, pp. 178–82.

Flora, J.A., Maibach, E.W. & Maccoby, N. 1989, 'The role of media across four levels of health promotion intervention', *Annual Review of Public Health*, vol. 10, pp. 181–201.

Fox, K.F. 1986, 'The measurement of issue/advocacy advertising effects', *Current Issues in Research in Advertising*, vol. 9, pp. 61–92.

Fox, K. & Kotler, P. 1980, 'Marketing of social causes: the first 10 years', *Journal of Marketing*, vol. 44, pp. 24–33.

France, A., Donovan, R.J., Watson, C. & Leivers, S. 1991, 'A chlamydia awareness campaign aimed at reducing HIV risks in young adults', *Australian Health Promotion Journal*, vol. 1, no. 1, pp. 19–28.

Freedman, J.L. 1984, 'Effect of television violence on aggressiveness', *Psychological Bulletin*, vol. 96, pp. 227–46.

Freimuth, V.S., Hammond, S.L. & Stein, J.A. 1988 'Health advertising: prevention for profit', *American Journal of Public Health*, vol. 78, pp. 557–61.

Freimuth, V.S. & Mettger, W. 1990, 'Is there a hard-to-reach audience?', *Public Health Reports*, vol. 105, pp. 232–8.

FTC news summary 1981, 'Tobacco industry spent more than $1 billion in 1979 to promote cigarette sales', 11 September, p. 1.

Gallanter, R. 1977, 'To the victim belongs the flaws', *American Journal of Public Health*, vol. 67, p. 1025.

Garrard, J. 1992, 'Promoting health and evaluating change', *Health Issues*, vol. 3, pp. 2–6.

Ghorpade, S. 1986, 'Agenda setting: a test of advertising's neglected function', *Journal of Advertising*, vol. 26, pp. 23–7.

Glantz, K. 1985, 'Nutrition education for risk factor reduction and patient education: a review', *Preventive Medicine*, vol. 14, pp. 721–52.

Gowers, S.E. 1954, *The Complete Plain Words*, HMP, London.

Green, L.W. & Kreuter, M.W. 1990, 'Health promotion as a public health strategy for the 1990s', *Annual Review of Public Health*, vol. 11, pp. 319–34.

Green, L.W., Kreuter, M.W., Deeds, S.G. & Partridge, K.B. 1980, *Health Education Planning: A Diagnostic Approach*, Mayfield Publishing, Palo Alto.

Green, L.W. & McAlister, A.L. 1984, 'Macrointervention to support health behavior: some theoretical perspectives and practical reflections', *Health Education Quarterly*, vol. 11, no. 3, pp. 332–9.

Griffiths, W. & Knutson, A. 1960, 'The role of the mass media in public health', *American Journal of Public Health*, vol. 50, pp. 515–23.

Grossman, S.A. 1992, 'Public sentiment affects health care reform', *The Academy Bulletin*, Academy for Health Services Marketing, July.

Hall, J., Heller, R., Dobson, A., Lloyd, D., Sanson-Fisher, R. & Leader, S. 1988, 'A cost effectiveness analysis of alternative strategies for the prevention of heart disease', *Medical Journal of Australia*, vol. 148, pp. 273–7.

Hastings, G. & Haywood, A. 1991, 'Social marketing and communication in health promotion', *Health Promotion International*, vol. 6, pp. 135–45.

Hawe, P., Degeling, D. & Hall, J. 1990, *Evaluating Health Promotion: A Health Worker's Guide*, MacLennan & Petty, Sydney.

Hetzel, B.S. & McMichael, A. 1983, *The LS Factor*, Allen & Unwin, Sydney.

Higbee, K.L. 1969, 'Fifteen years of fear arousal. Research on threat appeals: 1953–68', *Psychological Bulletin*, vol. 72, pp. 426–39.

Hinman, A.R. 1990, '1889 to 1989: A century of health and disease', *Public Health Reports*, vol. 105, no. 4, pp. 374–80.

Hitchcock, P.J. (ed.) 1988, 'Research issues in human behaviour and sexually transmitted diseases in the AIDS era', American Society for Microbiology, Washington, DC.

Holman, D. 1992, 'The political arithmetic of public health', *Health Promotion Journal of Australia*, vol. 2, no. 1, pp. 4–6.

Houston, F.S. & Gassenheimer, J.B. 1987, 'Marketing and exchange', *Journal of Marketing*, vol. 51, pp. 3–18.

Hugentobler, M. 1991, *Health Education Quarterly*, Summer, pp. 253–6.

Hyman, H. & Sheatsley, P. 1947, 'Some reasons why information campaigns fail', *Public Opinion Quarterly*, vol. 11, pp. 412–23.

Ivest, T. 1988, 'Ingenious campaign reinstates sugar as the natural sweetener', *Financial Review*, October, p. 11.

Janz, N. & Becker, M. 1984, 'The health belief model: a decade later', *Health Education Quarterly*, vol. 11, pp. 1–47.

Job, R.F.S. 1988, 'Effective and ineffective use of fear in health promotion campaigns', *American Journal of Public Health*, vol. 78, no. 2, pp. 163–7

Jordan, L. 1982, *The* New York Times *Style Book for Writers and Editors*, McGraw-Hill, New York.

Jung, C. 1964, *Man and His Symbols*, Dell Publishing, New York.

Kegeles, S. 1963, 'Some problems for the use of mass communication for public health', *Health Education Journal*, vol. 21, pp. 29–35.

Kelley, H.H. 1958, 'Salience of membership and resistance to change of group anchored attitudes', *Human Relations*, vol. 8, pp. 275–89.

Klapper, J.T. 1961, *The Effects of Mass Communication*, The Free Press, Glencoe, Ill.

Klare, G.R. 1976, 'A second look at the validity of readability formulas', *Journal of Reading Behavior*, vol. 8, pp. 129–52.

Koskela, K., McAlister, A., Kottke, T.E., Maccoby, N. & Farquhar, J.W. 1985, 'The community-based strategy to prevent heart disease: conclusions from the ten years of the North Karelia project', *Annual Review of Public Health*, vol. 6, pp. 147–93.

Kotler, P. & Andreasen, A.R. 1987, *Strategic Marketing for Nonprofit Organisations*, Prentice Hall, Englewood Cliffs, NJ.

Kotler, P. & Roberto, E.L. 1989, *Social Marketing: Strategies for Changing Public Behavior*, The Free Press, New York.

Kotler, P. 1988, *Marketing Management: Analysis, Planning, Implementation and Control*, Prentice Hall, Englewood Cliffs, NJ.

Kotler, P. 1989, *Principles of Marketing*, Prentice Hall, Englewood Cliffs, NJ.

Kotler, P. & Zaltman, G. 1971, 'Social marketing: an approach to planned social change', *Journal of Marketing*, vol. 35, pp. 3–12.

Krueger, R.A. 1988, *A Practical Guide for Applied Research*, Sage Publications, San Francisco.

Lancaster, K.J. 1966, 'A new approach to consumer theory', *Journal of Political Economy*, vol. 14, pp. 132–57.

Lancaster, W., McIlwain, T. & Lancaster, J. 1983, 'Health marketing: implications for health promotion', *Family and Community Health*, vol. 5, pp. 41–51.

Lasswell, H.D. 1948, 'The structure and function of communication in society' in Bryson, L. (ed.), *The Communication of Ideas*, Harper, New York, pp. 37–51.

LeFebvre, C. (1992), 'The social marketing imbroglio in health promotion', *Health Promotion International*, vol. 7, pp. 61–4.

Lefebvre, R.C. & Flora, J.A. 1988, 'Social marketing and public health intervention', *Health Education Quarterly*, vol. 15, pp. 299–315.

Levitt, T. 1969, *The Marketing Mode*, McGraw-Hill, New York.

Lewis, C.L., Sims, L.R. & Shannon, B. 1989, 'Examination of specific nutrition/health behaviors using a social cognitive model', *Journal of the American Dietetic Association*, vol. 89, no. 2, pp. 194–202.

Lord, C.G., Ross, L. & Lepper, M.R. 1979, 'Biased assimilation and attitude polarisation: the effects of prior theories on subsequently altered evidence', *Journal of Personality and Social Psychology*, vol. 37, pp. 2098–109.

Lunn, T. 1986, 'Segmenting and constructing markets' in Worcester, R.M. & Downham, J. (eds), *Consumer Market Research Handbook*, Amsterdam, North Holland, pp. 287–424.

Maccoby, N. & Alexander, J. 1980, 'Use of media in lifestyle programs', in Davidson, P. & Davidson, S. (eds), *Behavioral Medicine: Changing Health Lifestyles*, Brunel-Mazel, New York.

Maccoby, N., Farquhar, J., Wood, P.D. & Alexander, J. 1977, 'Reducing the risk of cardiovascular disease: effects of a community-based campaign on knowledge and behaviour', *Journal of Community Health*, vol. 3, no. 2, pp. 100–14.

Mackay, H. 1986, 'Teenagers', The Mackay Report, Sydney.

Macro Systems, 1987. Review of media, communication, and evaluation methodology literature. Prepared for US Public Health Service and the Centres for Disease Control, AIDS Information and Education Program.

Madigan, S. 1983 in Yuille, J.C. (ed.), *Imagery, Memory and Cognition*, Lawrence Erlbaum, New York.

Manoff, R.K. 1985, *Social Marketing*, Praeger, New York.

Marketing News, 1985, 'AMA board approves new marketing definition', 1 March, p. 1.

Maslow, A.H. 1968, *Toward a Theory of Being*, 2nd edn, Van Nostrand, New York.

McGuire, W. 1985, 'The myth of massive media impact: savagings and salvagings', in Rice, R.E. & Atkin, C.K. (eds), *Public Communication Campaigns*, Sage Publications, San Francisco.

McGuire, W.J. 1985, 'Attitudes and attitude change' (pp. 233–346), in *The Handbook of Social Psychology*, vol. II, Lindszey, G. & Aronson, E. (eds), 3rd edn, Random House, New York.

McGuire, W.J. 1984, 'Public communication as a strategy for inducing health-promoting behaviour change', *Preventive Medicine*, vol. 13, pp. 299–319.

McGuire, W.J. 1986, 'The myth of massive media impact: savagings and salvagings', *Public Communications and Behaviour*, vol. 1, pp. 173–220.

McKay, K. & Gasal, E. 1992, 'Clean-up Australia day', *Health Promotion Journal of Australia*, vol. 2, no. 2, p. 62.

McKee, N. 1992, *Social Mobilisation and Social Marketing*, Southbound, Penang, Malaysia.

McLuhan, M. 1964, *Understanding Media; The Extensions of Man*, McGraw-Hill, New York.

Mendehlson, H. 1973, 'Some reasons why information campaigns can succeed', *Public Opinion Quarterly*, vol. 37, pp. 50–61.

Merton, R.K. & Kendall, P. 1946, 'The focused interview', *American Journal of Sociology*, vol. 51, pp. 541–57.

Milio, N. 1986, 'Health and the media in Australia—an uneasy relationship', *Community Health Studies*, vol. 10, no. 4, pp. 419–22.

Miller, M. & Ware, J. 1989, *Mass media alcohol and drug campaigns: consideration of relevant issues*, Monograph Series No. 9, AGPS, Canberra.

Montgomery, K.C. 1990, 'Promoting health through entertainment television', in Atkin, C. & Wallack L. (eds), *Mass Communication and Public Health: Complexities and Conflicts*, Sage Publications, San Francisco.

Morgan, D.L. 1988, *Focus Groups as Qualitative Research*, Sage Publications, San Francisco.

Murphy, P.E. 1984, 'Analysing markets', in Frederiksen, L.W., Solomon, L.J. & Myers-Levy, J. 1988, 'The influence of sex roles on judgement', *Journal of Consumer Research*, vol. 14, pp. 522–30.

National Cancer Institute, 1982, *Pretesting in Health Communications* (NIH publication no. 83–1493), US Government Printing Office, Washington, DC.

National Centre for Health Statistics, 1988, *Advance Data on AIDS*, NCDC, Atlanta.

National Institute of Health, 1982, *Television and Behaviour: Ten Years of Scientific Progress and Implications for the Eighties*, Government Printing Office, Washington, DC.

Neuendorf, K.A. 1987, 'Alcohol and advertising: evidence from social science', *Media Information Australia*, no. 43.

Nissinen, A., Koskela, K. & Takalo, T. 1979, 'Changes in coronary risk factors during comprehensive five-year community programme to control cardiovascular disease (the North Karelia project)', *British Medical Journal*, vol. 2, pp. 1173–8.

Noelle-Neumann, E. 1974, 'Spiral of silence: a theory of public opinion', *Journal of Communications*, vol. 24, pp. 43–51.

Novelli, W.D. 1984, 'Developing marketing programs', in Frederickson, L.W., Solomon, L.J. & Brehony, K.A. (eds), *Marketing Health Behavior: Principles, Techniques and Applications*, Plennum, New York.

O'Keefe, D.J. 1990, *Persuasion: Theory and Research*, Sage Publications, San Francisco.

Ornstein, R.E. 1975, *The Psychology of Consciousness*, Harcourt Brace Jovanovich, San Diego.

Ornstein, R.E. 1986, *Multi Mind*, McMillan, London.

Pelto, G.H. 1981, 'Anthropological contributions to nutrition education research', *Journal of Nutrition Education*, vol. 13, p. 2.

Percy, L. & Rossiter, J.R. 1978, *Advertising Strategy: A Communications Approach*, Praeger, New York.

Powles, J. 1973, 'On the limitations of modern medicine', *Science, Medicine and Man*, vol. 1, pp. 1–30.

Pride, W.M. & Ferrell, O.C. 1980, *Marketing: Basic Concepts and Decisions*, Houghton Mifflin, Boston.

Prochaska, J.O. 1991, 'Assessing how people change', *Cancer*, vol. 67, pp. 805–8.

Puska, P., Toumilehto, J., Salonen, J., Neittaanmaki, L., Maki, J. & Virtamo, J. 1985, 'The community based strategy to prevent heart disease: conclusions of the ten years of the North Karelia project', *Annual Review of Public Health*, vol. 6, pp. 147–93.

Puska, P., McAlister, A., Niemwnsivu, H., Piha, T., Wiilo, J. et al. 1987, 'A television format for national health promotion: Finland's "Keys to Health" ', *Public Health Reports*, 1987, vol. 102, pp. 263–9.

Puska, P., McAlister, A., Pekkola, J. & Koskela, K. 1981, 'Television in health promotion: evaluation of a national programme in Finland', *International Journal of Health Education*, vol. 24, pp. 2–14.

Puska, P., Wiio, J., McAlister, A., Koskela, K., Smolander, A., Pekkola, J. & Maccoby, N. 1985a, 'Planned use of mass media in national health promotion: the "Keys to Health" TV program in 1982 in Finland', *Canadian Journal of Public Health*, vol. 76, pp. 336–42.

Puska, P., Nissinen, A., Tuomilehto, J., Salonen, J. & Koskela, K. 1985b, 'The community based strategy to prevent coronary heart disease: conclusion from the ten years of the North Karelia project', vol. 6, pp. 147–93.

Ramirez, A.G. & McAlister, A.L. 1988, 'Mass media campaign: a su salud', *Preventive Medicine*, vol. 17, pp. 608–21.

Redman, S., Spencer, E.A. & Sanson-Fisher, R. 1990, 'The role of mass media in changing health related behaviour: a critical appraisal of two models', *Health Promotion International*, vol. 5, pp. 85–101.

Research Triangle Institute, 1990, 'Feasibility study regarding paid advertising: evaluation design studies'. Report to Centers for Disease Control, contract no. 200-88-0643.

Reznick, R., Morey, S. & Best, J. 1984, *Medical Journal of Australia*, vol. 141, pp. 818–21.

Rickard, G.L. 1992, 'Focus group interviewing: an underutilized evaluation technique in physical education research', *The Physical Educator*, vol. 49, no. 1, pp. 1–5.

Rice, R.E. & Atkin, K.J. 1989, *Public Communication Campaigns*, Sage Publications, San Francisco.

Rice, R.E. & Paisley, W.J. (eds) 1981, *Public Communication Campaigns*, Sage Publications, Newbury Park, CA.

Rippertoe, P.A. & Rogers, R.W. 1987, 'Effects of components of protection-motivation theory on adaptive and maladaptive coping with a health threat', *Journal of Personality and Social Psychology*, vol. 52, pp. 596–604.

Rissel, C. 1991a, 'Using the media for health promotion: a continuing discussion', *Health Promotion Journal of Australia*, vol. 1, no. 2, pp. 64–5.

Rissel, C. 1991b, 'What are people like who respond to TV offers for further information? The case of the "Bodyshow" series', *Australian Journal of Public Health*, vol. 15, no. 1, pp. 43–8.

Roberts, D. & Maccoby, N. 1985, 'Information processing and persuasion; counterarguing behaviour' in Clarke, P. (ed.), *New Models for Mass Communication Research*, Sage Publications, San Francisco.

Rogers, E. 1983, *Diffusion of Innovations*, 3rd edn, Free Press, New York.

Rogers, E.M. & Storey, J.D. 1987, 'Communication campaigns', in Berget, C.R. & Chattee, S.H. (eds), *Handbook of Communication Science*, Sage Publications, San Francisco.

Rogers, E. & Shoemaker, F. 1971, *Communication of Innovations: A Cross Cultural Approach*, Free Press, New York.

Rogers. R.W. 1975, 'A protection motivation theory of fear appeals and attitude change', *Journal of Psychology*, vol. 91, pp. 93–114.

Rogers, R.W. 1983 'Cognitive and physiological process in fear appeals and attitude change: a revised theory of protection motivation', in Cacioppo, J. & Petty, R. (eds), *Social Psychophysiology*, Guilford Press, New York.

Rose, G. 1985, 'Sick individuals and sick populations', *International Journal of Epidemiology*, vol. 14, no. 1, pp. 32–8.

Rosenstock, I., Strecher, V. & Becker, M. 1988, 'Social learning theory and the health belief model', *Health Education Quarterly*, vol. 15, pp. 175–83.

Rosenstock, I.M. 1974, *Historical Origins of the Health Belief Model*, Health Education Monographs, no. 2, pp. 409–19.

Rossiter, J.R. 1989, 'Market segmentation: a review and proposed resolution', *Australian Marketing Researcher*, vol. 11, pp. 36–58,.

Rossiter, J.R. & Donovan, R.J. 1983, 'Why you shouldn't test ads in focus groups', *Australian Marketing Researcher*, vol. 7, pp. 43–8.

Rossiter, J., Percy, L. & Donovan, R.J. 1984, 'The advertising plan and advertising communication models', *Australian Marketing Researcher*, vol. 8, pp. 7–44.

Rossiter, J.R. & Percy, L. 1987, *Advertising and Promotion Management*, McGraw-Hill, New York.

Rothschild, M.L. 1979, 'Marketing communications in non-business situations or why it's so hard to sell brotherhood like soap', *Journal of Marketing*, vol. 43, pp. 11–20.

Routt, D.C. & Schneidler, R. 1992, 'Regional public education program tackles reform questions', *The Academy Bulletin*, Academy for Health Services Marketing, July.

Rubinstein, P. 1987, 'Food advertising', in Wahlqvist, M., King, R.W., McNeil, J. & Sewell, R. (eds), *Food and Health: Issues and Directions*, John Libbey, London.

Sammon, K. 1987, *Planning for Out-of-Home Media*, The Traffic Audit Bureau, New York.

Schiffman, L.G. & Kanuk, L.L. 1983, *Consumer Behaviour*, Prentice Hall, Englewood Cliffs, NJ.

Sheth, J.N. & Frazier, G.L. 1982, 'A model of strategy mix choice for planned social change', *Journal of Marketing*, vol. 46, pp. 15–26.

Sims, L.S. 1987, 'Nutrition education research: reaching toward the leading edge', *Journal of the American Dietetic Association*, vol. 87 (Supplement): S–10.

Singhal, A. & Rogers, E.M. 1989, 'Prosocial television for development in India', in Rice, R.E. & Atkin, C.K. (eds), *Public Communication Campaigns*, Sage Publications, San Francisco.

Sirgy, M.J., Morris, M. & Samli, A.C. 1985, 'The question of value in social marketing: use of a quality-of-life theory to achieve long-term satisfaction', *American Journal of Economics and Sociology*, vol. 44, pp. 215–28.

Siska, M., Jason, J., Murdoch, P., Yang, W.S. & Donovan, R.J. 1992, 'Recall of AIDS public service announcements and their impact on the ranking of AIDS as a national problem', *American Journal of Public Health*, vol. 82, pp. 1029–32.

Slater, M.D. & Flora, J.A. 1989, 'Health lifestyles: audience segmentation analysis for public health interventions', *Health Education Quarterly*, vol. 18, pp. 221–3.

Smith, W. 1956, 'Product differentiation and market segmentation as alternative marketing strategies', *Journal of Marketing*, vol. 21, no. 1, pp. 3–8.

Solomon, D.S. 1982, 'Mass media campaigns in health promotion', *Prevention in Human Services*, vol. 2, nos 1 and 2, pp. 115–23.

Solomon, D.S. 1989, 'A social marketing perspective on communication campaigns', in Rice, R.E. & Atkin, C.K. (eds), *Public Communication Campaigns*, Sage Publications, San Francisco.

Solomon, D.S. 1984, 'Social marketing and community health promotion: the Stanford heart disease prevention program', in Frederiksen, L.W., Solomon, L.J. & Brehony, K.A. (eds), *Marketing Health Behaviour*, Plennum Press, New York.

Solomon, D.S. 1981, 'A social marketing perspective on campaigns', in Rice, R.E. & Paisley W.J. (eds), *Public Communication Campaigns*, Sage Publications, San Francisco.

Spark, R. & Mills, P. 1988, 'Promoting Aboriginal health on television in the Northern Territory: a bicultural approach', *Drug Education Journal of Australia*, vol. 2, no. 3, pp. 191–8.

Spark, R., Donovan, R.J. & Howat, P. 1991, 'Promoting health and preventing injury in remote Aboriginal communities: a case study', *Health Promotion Journal of Australia*, vol. 1, no. 2, pp. 10–16.

Spark, R., Binns, C., Laughlin, D., Spooner, C. & Donovan, R.J. 1992, 'Aboriginal people's perceptions of their own and their community's health: results of a pilot study', *Health Promotion Journal of Australia*, vol. 2, no. 2, pp. 60–4.

Strickland, B.R. 1978, 'Internal–external expectancies and health related behaviour', *Journal of Consulting and Clinical Psychology*, vol. 46, pp. 1192–291.

Strunk, W. & White, E.B. 1971, *The Elements of Style*, 2nd edn, Macmillan, New York.

Sturm, A. 1992, 'Hospital advocacy campaign informs consumers, voters', *The Academy Bulletin*, Academy for Health Services Marketing, July.

Sutton, S.R. 1982, 'Fear-arousing communications: a critical examination of theory and research', in Eiser, J.R. (ed.), *Social Psychology and Behavioural Medicine*, John Wiley, New York.

Szlichcinski, K.P. 1980, in Kolers, P.A. et al. (eds), *Processing of Visible Language*, Plennum Press, New York.

Tones, B.K. 1977, 'Effectiveness and efficiency in health education'. Occasional paper produced for the Scottish Health Education Unit.

Tye, J.B., Warner, K.E. & Glantz, S. 1988, 'Tobacco advertising and consumption: evidence of a causal relationship', *World Smoking and Health*, Winter.

Vidmar, N. & Rokeach, M. 1974, 'Archie Bunker's bigotry: a study in selective perception and exposure', *Journal of Communication*, vol. 24, pp. 36–47.

Vingilis, E. & Coultes, B. 1990, 'Mass communications and drinking-driving: theories, practice and results', *Alcohol, Drugs and Driving*, vol. 6, pp. 61–81.

Wallack, L. & Dorfman, L. 1992, 'Health messages on television commercials', *American Journal of Health Promotion*, vol. 6, pp. 190–6.

Wallack, L. 1990a, 'Media advocacy: promoting health through mass communications', in Glanz, K., Lewis, F.M. & Rimer, B.K. (eds), *Health Behaviour and Health Education:*

Theory, Research and Practice, Jossey-Bass, San Francisco.

Wallack, L. 1990b, 'Improving health promotion: media advocacy and social marketing approaches', in Atkin, C. & Wallach, L. (eds), *Mass Communication and Public Health. Complexities and Conflicts*, Sage Publications, San Francisco.

Wallack, L. 1985, 'The prevention of alcohol related problems in the USA: health educators and the "new generation" of "strategies" ', *Hygiene*, vol. 4, p. 26.

Wallack, L. 1989, 'Mass communication and health promotion: a critical perspective', in Rice, R.E. & Paisley, W.I. (eds), *Public Communication Campaigns*, Sage Publications, San Francisco.

Wallack, L.M. 1983, 'Mass media campaigns in a hostile environment: advertising as anti health education', *Journal of Alcohol and Drug Education*, vol. 28, no. 2, pp. 51–62.

Wallack, L.M. 1980, 'Assessing effects of mass media campaigns: an alternative perspective', *Alcohol, Health and Research World*, Fall, pp. 17–29.

Warner, K.E. 1987, 'Television and health education: stay tuned', *American Journal of Public Health*, vol. 77, pp. 140–2.

White, S.L. & Maloney, S.K. 1990, 'Promoting healthy diets and active lives to hard-to-reach groups: market research study', Public Health Reports, vol. 105, pp. 224–31.

Whitehead, P.C. 1979, 'Public policy and alcohol related damage: media campaigns or social controls', *Addictive Behaviours*, vol. 4, pp. 83–9.

Wiebe, G. 1952, 'Merchandising commodities and citizenship on television', *Public Opinion Quarterly*, vol. 15, pp. 679–91.

Wilde, G.J.S. & Ackersviller, M.J. 1981, 'Accident journalism and traffic safety education', Transport Canada, Traffic Safety Report no. TP 3659 E/CR 8202, Ottawa.

Wilde, G.J.S. 1992, 'Effects of mass media communications upon health and safety habits of individuals: an overview of issues and evidence'. Unpublished paper, Department of Psychology, Queen's University, Canada.

Willard, N. 1986, 'Selling healthy behaviour: success and failures', in Leathar, D.S., Hastings, G.B., O'Reilly, K.M. & Davies, J.K. (eds), *Health Education and the Media II*, Pergamon Press, Oxford.

Williams, B.T. 1984, 'Are public health education campaigns worthwhile?', *British Medical Journal*, vol. 288, pp. 170–1.

Winnett, R.A., King, A.C. & Altman, D.G. 1990, 'Extending applications of behavior therapy to large scale intervention', in Martin, P.R. (ed.), *Handbook of Behavior Therapy and Psychological Science: An Integrative Approach*, Pergamon, New York, pp. 473–90.

Woods, D.R., Davis, D. & Westover, B.J. 1991, 'America responds to AIDS: its content, development process, and outcome', *Public Health Reports*, vol. 106, pp. 616–22.

World Health Organisation, 1983, 'Health education in primary care', *World Health Organisation Journal*, vol. 2, no. 1, pp. 170–1.

Wright, J.S., Winter, W.L. & Zeigler, S.K. 1982, *Advertising*, McGraw-Hill, New York.

Young, E. 1989, 'Social marketing in the information era'. American Marketing Association Conference, Social Marketing for the 1990s, Ottawa, Canada.

Zimbardo, P., Ebbersen, E. & Malasch, C. 1977, *Influencing Attitudes and Changing Behavior*, Addison-Wesley, Melo-Park, CA.

Index

Page numbers in *italics* refer to illustrations. Page numbers in **bold type** refer to main entries.